D1453147

BLACK BREAD AND BARBED WIRE

BLACK BREAD AND BARBED WIRE

Prisoners in the First World War

EDITED BY

MICHAEL MOYNIHAN

LEO COOPER · LONDON

0429509 ~~109643~~

First published in Great Britain 1978 by
LEO COOPER LTD.,
196 Shaftesbury Avenue,
London WC2H 8JL

Copyright © 1978 The Imperial War Museum
ISBN 0 85052 239 00

Set in 10 on 12 pt 'Monotype' Times Roman
and printed in Great Britain by
Ebenezer Baylis and Son Ltd
The Trinity Press, Worcester, and London

CONTENTS

0429509 ~~109643~~

ACKNOWLEDGEMENTS

I am greatly indebted to the Imperial War Museum for access to their archives. In particular I would like to thank Mr Roderick Suddaby, Head of the Department of Documents, for his expert assistance in selecting material, and the Library staff for help with research.

I am much obliged for the illuminating commentaries on their experiences in PoW camps provided by Mr Norman Dykes and Mr George Waymark, and for the background information supplied by the relatives and acquaintances of former Able Seaman J. C. Farrant, Leading Seaman E. Surrey Dane, Rifleman E. Evanson, Captain D. Lyall Grant MC, and RQMS F. A. Harvey, and by Mr V. C. Coombs, Hon. Secretary, Officer Prisoner of War (1914–18) Dining Club.

Finally I owe a debt of gratitude to the Editor of *The Sunday Times*, Mr Harold Evans, without whose support and encouragement work on this book would not have been possible, and grateful thanks are also due to Mr Magnus Linklater, Assistant Editor (News).

M.M.

FOREWORD

APART FROM A spate of first-hand accounts published in the 1920s and long since out of print, almost nothing has been written about the 6,482 British officers and 163,907 other ranks who were taken prisoner in the First World War. This book is an often startling revelation of what went on in that limbo the wrong side of No Man's Land.

Black Bread and Barbed Wire is the fifth book I have edited from the diaries, letters and journals of ordinary participants in the two World Wars, either acquired by the Imperial War Museum or sent to *The Sunday Times*, following an invitation to readers. Particularly in the case of the First World War, it is only in recent years that such illuminating individual accounts have come to light, many of them discovered gathering dust in attics following the deaths of those who wrote them.

When Roderick Suddaby, Head of the Department of Documents at the Imperial War Museum, suggested that enough material was now available for a book on First World War prisoners of war, it seemed at first a dubious project, even if breaking new ground. Would it not be a recital of suffocating boredom? A reading of the dozens of diaries and journals from which these seven have been chosen quickly dispelled that notion. Grindingly monotonous the actual experiences of life behind barbed wire may often have been. But, as chronicled by a diversity of individuals, they had a hypnotic readability.

What most notably emerges is a new concept of courage. Far from the spotlight of the fighting front, the silent battles being waged in these drab backwaters of war were against degradation and despair, physical collapse and mental stagnation. They were battles in which the chief enemy could be oneself, and with which we may more readily identify than with those much-documented battles long ago waged with bullet and bayonet.

There are horror stories enough in the accounts that follow. Stories of men reduced to near skeletons; of men trussed tip-toe to posts with hands above their heads as punishment for trivial offences; of men working naked in the suffocating heat of coal mines, or freezing (sometimes to death) as slave labour in German trenches on the Russian front; of men driven to self-immolation, to madness, to suicide. Most appalling of all is RQMS Harvey's diary of a death march across the scorching deserts of Mesopotamia under the whips of mounted Kurdish guards, whose sadism was only equalled by the Japanese in the Second World War.

In an age attuned to violence such brutalities may have a blunted impact. What could be more immediately shocking to egalitarian susceptibilities is the revelation of the kid glove treatment accorded to officers and which they accepted as no more than their due. After the siege of Kut in Mesopotamia in 1916, for example, it was taken for granted that the officers should go one way to a comparatively comfortable captivity, the half-starved other ranks along a Via Dolorosa which only the toughest were to survive.

Even accepting that the privileges of rank are integral to the military ethos, it is difficult to feel an equal sympathy for the well-fed officers in German PoW camps portrayed in Captain Lyall Grant's voluminous diary: preoccupied with organized games, theatricals, language classes, private parties, waited on hand and foot by British orderlies who counted this double servitude a blessing by comparison with the rigours of their own primitive camps.

But it is necessary to recognize (as indicated by Norman Dykes, who served a spell as 'Private Jeeves') that other-rank PoWs themselves found nothing strange or reprehensible in this state of affairs. Within the disciplines of the army, they accepted it as being as much in the natural order of things as had been the Upstairs-Downstairs class structure of the Edwardian England they had grown up in. It is also necessary to recognize that enforced idleness could prove quite as intolerable as enforced labour.

The officers' ordeal is summed up in one of the few general accounts of life in officer PoW camps (*Comrades in Captivity* by F. W. Harvey), published in 1920:

> 'What use are you to this camp?' That was the unasked question which had to be answered by every new arrival. It was hard, rank Socialism, but very successful. You lived for the State, not for yourself. Something you *must* do to keep the life of the camp alight. Something you *must* do, or be damned . . .
>
> Herein at least soldiers, brutally forced to work in factories or salt mines or more pleasantly on farms, score over their officers compelled to idleness, except they make employment for themselves and for one another. 'God give me forgetfulness!' has been the prayer of many a man driven morbid and mad by this terrible inactivity.

Today most people's conception of the British fighting man in captivity relates almost exclusively to the Second World War and is coloured by semi-fictionalized films like *The Wooden Horse* and the BBC's TV series *Colditz*, in which young officers spend most of their time planning ingenious methods of escape. Other-rank PoWs, whose experiences could be little less grim than their First World War counterparts, have not been rated a box-office attraction, with the notable exception of the disciplined skeletons in *The Bridge on the River Kwai*.

192,319 British prisoners were taken in the Second World War,

170,389 in the First. Why is it that the fate of a total 362,708 servicemen, often suffering greater hardships than those at the front, has gone virtually unrecognized, while books and films about the fighting in both wars continue to proliferate?

An element of shame (usually quite unjustified) that has attached itself to the fighting man who holds up his hands in surrender might have had much to do with this 'out-of-sight, out-of-mind' attitude. And for PoWs themselves it was inevitably a shameful experience to find themselves unarmed and totally at the mercy of their enemy. How to hit back was the preoccupation of all but those who succumbed to sickness or inertia.

To escape was the positive way to do so, and, because most books and films by and about PoWs have been escape stories, a quite erroneous impression has built up that PoW camps were hotbeds of conspiracy. In fact (as shown in Chapter 3) escapees were a breed apart, comparatively few in number and mostly officers (with leisure enough to hatch plots). For most prisoners 'outwitting the Bosche' was the great morale-booster, a battle of wits (zestfully described by Leading Seaman Surrey Dane) which could range from 'dodging the column' to the sabotage of factory machinery or that most potent of weapons against the 'humourless Hun', mockery.

The majority of PoWs, indeed, had little to be ashamed of in their conduct under the enemy yoke. But neither was it something to boast about on their eventual release. Memories of that purgatorial existence behind barbed wire were like a bad dream you blink away on waking. It is significant that the families of two former PoWs whose diaries are posthumously featured in this book were quite unaware of their existence.

The seven accounts that follow give vivid close-ups of a limbo unexplored by the historian. A brief background summary may set them in a clearer perspective.

At the outbreak of the First World War the belligerent nations were bound by international law as to their treatment of prisoners. At the Geneva Convention of 1906 and the Hague Convention of 1907 all the major European countries had agreed that humane treatment was obligatory, and that restricted punishment of prisoners was permissible for acts of insubordination. As the war progressed specific problems unforeseen by these Conventions arose, and a series of bilateral agreements were reached between the belligerent powers, notably on the employment of other-rank PoWs as labourers (in agriculture, specified industries, transport and public utility services), and on the repatriation or exchange (by internment in neutral countries) of certain categories of wounded or sick prisoners and prisoners who had served long periods in captivity.

During the early stages of the war (as Chapters 1 and 2 testify) the Germans, confident of early victory, felt at liberty to ignore all agreements. Thereafter the treatment of prisoners was largely determined by the dictates of the Camp Commandant and by the efficacy of the pressures brought to bear on the German authorities by visiting teams of neutral observers.

For most prisoners food (or the lack of it) was the constant obsession. The inadequacy of the German ration of black bread, watery soup and ersatz coffee, is the dominant theme of every account by other-rank PoWs. But here it should be noted that this near-starvation diet was not just another example of German 'frightfulness'. For Britain as well as Germany it soon became clear that it was not possible to stick to the terms of the Geneva Convention, which stipulated that PoWs should be fed equivalent rations to those of their own troops. Between them, the Allied blockade and the German submarine campaign were necessitating ever more stringent rationing for the civilian populations, and riots must have followed any disclosure that enemy prisoners were being cosseted.

The vital lifeline for every British PoW was the food parcel from home. For officers, into whose camps a constant stream of parcels poured, they constituted the staple diet, the unpalatable German black bread being regarded as a 'punishment' in emergencies, or something to store as a bribe for a camp guard. For other ranks they could mean the difference between life and death.

Few of their families could afford much from their own meagre rations, and, as the plight of prisoners became known, voluntary organizations sprang up throughout the country to keep prisoners supplied with essential nutriment. From fund-raising bazaars to public meetings addressed by escaped PoWs, this dedicated campaign was undoubtedly instrumental in saving the lives of many who would otherwise have died from diseases due to malnutrition, if not outright starvation.

It should be finally recognized that, grim as was the lot of the British other-rank PoW, it was scarcely comparable with that of those other allied prisoners, particularly the Russians, who received no food parcels from home and had been virtually abandoned by their governments. Numerically the British PoWs were a tiny fraction of a total running into many hundreds of thousands, the majority (as in the Second World War) captured on the Russian front.

There is a macabre footnote to history to be found in Captain Lyall Grant's diary entry at Gütersloh Camp in August, 1916: 'Tennis today with two Russians, one of whom owns a little place in Russia, about half the size of France, and wants me to go there after the war for some bear hunting . . .' A year later the Bolshevik Revolution was to change all that. But, whatever became of their officers, the fate of countless numbers of potential Comrades in other-rank camps had already been sealed – death by starvation. The grimmest memories of former other-rank PoWs I have spoken to are of those starving Russian contingents attached to their camps. 'Like beaten curs,' says Norman Dykes, 'pathetically hanging round our gates in the hope of scraps.'

It is not within the scope of this book to apportion guilt. But a contemporary judgement by an American may serve as evidence. It comes from a book published in America in 1919, *Prisoners of the Great War*, by Carl P. Dennett, who was American Red Cross Deputy Commissioner in Switzerland in 1917 and 1918. Responsible for the welfare of the trainloads of sick and wounded prisoners of every Allied nationality that poured into neutral Switzerland from Germany for internment or repatriation, Dennett had a unique opportunity of building up a picture of what was going on in German camps.

From time immemorial it has been the custom of the captor state to provide food and clothing for its prisoners of war. Germany, however, notoriously failed to even provide them with the bare necessities of life, and it is a fact beyond dispute that the ravages of disease due to malnutrition, and even starvation, have killed tens of thousands of prisoners in the hands of the German military forces. Other thousands have been interned in Switzerland, or repatriated to their homes, human wrecks as a result of the failure of the German Government to properly feed and clothe them. Neither treaty nor humanitarian consideration induced the German Government to treat its prisoners of war as human beings, or make much effort to preserve their lives. . . .

The treatment of prisoners of war in German prison camps goes hand in hand down the German path of terrorism with the asphyxiating gases, the incendiary bombs, the poisoned wells, the killings of innocent civilians, and can all be traced to the German teachings, and the certainty of the Germans that they could not be beaten and held responsible for their crimes.

Forgive and forget seems to have been the motto of most British PoWs after liberation. Retribution is only twice alluded to in the following pages. Able Seaman Farrant records having met a fellow prisoner after the war, a rugged North Sea fisherman, whose 'undying wish' was to meet up with the sadistic German corporal who had tied him up on one leg as a punishment, an ordeal from which he was still suffering after-effects. Chelsea Pensioner Ned Burwood's reaction was instantaneous when asked his feelings (after a lapse of 60 years) about the Kurdish guards on the death march from Kut: 'I'd shoot the buggers now if I had my way.' But, individuals apart, the general feeling was that most Germans (and Turks) were only carrying out orders, and that (towards the end of the war at least) they were faring little better than their captors so far as food, clothing and other commodities were concerned.

Most PoWs seek to forget their ordeals. But there is ample evidence that the hidden effects of deprivation, malnutrition and brutality can surface later in life. Research by ex-servicemen's associations has established many cases where former PoWs, after leading normal lives, have suffered mental or physical breakdowns when resistance declines in middle age. They claim that such cases are, in effect, belated 'war casualties', and should be entitled to disablement pensions.

This research has been largely concerned with Second World War PoWs. There is now no way of gauging how many veterans of the First World War may have died prematurely or become psychiatric cases as a result of their prison camp experiences. Carl Dennett describes one of the commonest complaints among PoWs reaching Switzerland in 1917 and 1918 as 'barbed-wire disease, a form of neurasthenia that became so prevalent and well defined that men were freed from German prison camps as unfit for further military duty because of it'. It seems unlikely that there would not have been lasting effects from such a breakdown, rooted in that most intangible of a prisoner's ordeals, 'deprivation'.

What must be read between the lines of every first-hand account of life behind barbed wire is the gnawing ache of separation from loved ones for an unforeseeable duration of time. In one of the magazines regularly produced in most officer PoW camps, whose contributions have about them an air of half-gallant, half-desperate jocularity, the opening lines of a poem by one officer sums it all up in a way that would be understood by every prisoner of every nationality in every camp:

> 'Walking round our cages like the lions at the Zoo,
> We see the phantom faces of you, and you,
> and you . . .'

Chapter One

FOUR YEARS' HARD LABOUR

ABLE SEAMAN JAMES FARRANT

AN OLD BROWN paper parcel, tied up with string and marked 'Prisoner of War', found among the effects of Eric Surrey Dane after his death in 1975 at the age of 80, was found to contain the fullest and most graphic accounts that have come to light of what it was like to be an other-rank prisoner of war of the Germans for almost the entire duration of the First World War.

The major part of the contents consisted of draft chapters and fragmentary notes written by Surrey Dane shortly after the war for an intended book. The pressures of business life halted work on what would have been a notable addition to the scant literature of First World War PoWs. Also in the package was a 30,000-word account by a fellow PoW, James Clifford Farrant, written up in 1919 from diaries he somehow managed to keep throughout his four years' captivity.

Leading Seaman Surrey Dane and Able Seaman Farrant had both joined the Royal Naval Volunteer Reserve some years before the war, and they were among the 3,000 men of the Royal Naval Division who were rushed to the assistance of the Belgian Army early in October, 1914, only to be captured after the fall of Antwerp. It was their misfortune to be captured at a time when the Germans were flushed with the prospect of an early victory and let loose on their helpless captors their indoctrinated hatred for the '*Englisch Schwein*'. Later it was their misfortune to be sent to Russia, pawns in a grim game of 'reprisals', where numbers of their fellow prisoners died of starvation, exposure and ill-treatment; others were driven mad.

Though not closely acquainted, both men came from similar middle-class backgrounds, and their accounts reveal the same qualities of tenacity and resourcefulness that were later to take them to the top in their chosen professions (Surrey Dane in commerce, Farrant in mining engineering). Though Farrant hints at near-despair during the freezing winter of 1917, when 600 British PoWs were made to work in the German trenches on the Russian front ('I don't know how much longer I can stick it—my strength has just about given out'), there is a remarkable buoyancy in their reactions to conditions and treatment that would have been unthinkable in officers' camps.

Both men held their German taskmasters in contempt. Farrant scathingly records that 'the Germans became more brutal to British prisoners of war during those periods when we were short of food, and were consequently weak from hunger'. During such periods prisoners could be reduced to the state of passive zombies. For the most part they lost no opportunity of registering defiance. Surrey Dane's unfinished journal is peppered with examples of 'outwitting the Hun', or 'dodging the column', and it is on these passages that Chapter 2 has been based.

As an historic record, Farrant's account has the advantage of being based on diary notes made at the time, written up into narrative form with only the occasional hindsight interpolation. Aged 29 at the outbreak of the war (nine years older than Surrey Dane), Farrant had risen to be London manager of a mining company, and, on his return after the Armistice, he was persuaded to write his account for *The Mining Magazine*. Appearing in eight monthly instalments in 1919, it was later reprinted as a booklet, entitled *Four Years as a Prisoner of War—Döberitz, Russia, Saxony*, a copy of which Farrant sent to Surrey Dane. It is thanks to William Surrey Dane, who found the two accounts in the attic of his brother Eric's home after his death, and who sent them to the Imperial War Museum, that the lid can be lifted, after 60 years, on First World War brutalities unrecorded in the history books.

How nearly Farrant's diary came to going the way of many another is recorded in a foreword to his account:

'On many occasions searches for diaries were made by the German authorities, but they did not find mine. On one occasion a diary kept by another prisoner was found when we were in the Russian trenches, with the result that the whole Company was punished by working an additional two hours daily. This made our men sore, and I was quite unpopular for a time because they knew I had a diary as well. I almost decided to destroy my notes, but on second thoughts I did not.'

Farrant died in 1966. The ensuing chapter is a posthumous justification of those second thoughts.

On the morning of 4 October, 1914, men of the Royal Naval Division at Walmer marched to Dover and embarked for Dunkirk, arriving there the following morning. We reached Antwerp early on the 6th, and marched to our positions. This affair has already been sufficiently discussed, but one fact, which is often overlooked, remains, namely that the entire Belgian Army was enabled to retire.

We were captured at Exarde on the night of the 9th. From Saturday, the 3rd, until the 10th, I had only eight hours sleep, and up to the time of our capture had marched continuously for 24 hours. Half an hour after our capture we were marching, or I should say stumbling along with our eyes closed, for we were all in, when we were fired upon, presumably by a German picket. Our guards made a dive for the hedges on either side of the road. So did we, with disastrous results, as a German officer screamed out we were trying to escape, whereupon our guards opened up at point blank range or else used their bayonets. A man next to me was bayonetted, and was left, as were others, in the ditches.

We arrived at a small church about 3 am on the 10th, where we were interned. Double guards were mounted in the pulpit, organ loft, and on the altar. We were crowded in any fashion. We were given a 1lb loaf between ten, and a cupful of soup on the following day. Ten men at a time were allowed to go to the latrine. Many men, as soon as they came in contact with the fresh air, rolled about like drunken men. There were about 1,000 all told in the church, British and Belgians, and at night two pails were placed in the church for urinal purposes. Imagine it! 1,000 men and two pails. The men sleeping on the floor near the pails were very tired – and wet.

On 12 October we were formed up and marched to Termonde, the prisoners carrying the guards' packs. At midday we halted, the guards pulling up some swedes, which we ate ravenously. We reached Termonde about 1 pm. While waiting at the railway siding, a German cook, who was operating a field cooker, hooked out a piece of meat and held it out to one of our men, who, upon approaching, just dodged a welt from a soup ladle, while the meat was given to a Belgian, much to the amusement of some German officers standing by.

We entrained about 3 pm in cattle trucks. The Belgians had straw in theirs, and 20 men to a truck. We had 40 men, and no straw. A further distinction was made with the aid of chalk on the Belgian trucks, where someone had written '*Belgian gut, Francosen gut, aber Englisch Schwein*'. At our first stopping place people crowded on the platform to see the *Englisch Schwein*, and the men and women were equally dexterous in expectorating at us. They changed guards, four to each cattle truck, at Cologne, which we reached at midnight. One slice of war bread per man was given us; it tasted like angel cake to me.

The next morning we pulled up at a station and coffee was brought to the guards. We had had nothing to drink since the previous day, so we asked the Red Cross female attendant who brought the guards' coffee to give us some. She merely used the well-worn expression '*schwein*', and deliberately poured the remaining coffee on the platform. We were 60 hours on this train, during which time we had one soup meal and one slice of bread. It was too cold to sleep, and only some of the men could lie down at one time.

We reached Döberitz [near Berlin] at 6 am on 15 October, all very cold. We were put in tents, three men on two mattresses, large rents in tents, and no fires. The tents, which held about 400 men, were erected on waste ground. The damp soon rotted the mattresses, which were filled with wood wool. The camp routine was: Reveille 5.30 am, coffee 6 am, work 6.30 am, soup 12 am, work 1 pm, coffee 6 pm. Besides the soup and coffee we received half of a 3-lb loaf per day.

At Döberitz there were two camps surrounded by barbed wire and divided by a road. In Camp No. 1 there were 4,000 Mons men, who were captured in August. We were given blankets, bowl and spoon. Our knives were taken from us, and we sharpened our spoon handles on stones in order to divide the bread. It was very cold. Most of the naval men only wore their flannels, having left their jerseys in their kit bags. Many of us tied blankets round our bodies, and then put our oilskins on top. It was rather an uncomfortable walking rig, but fairly warm.

The work consisted of general labouring. Cleaning out refuse bins in the German barracks fell to my lot for a whole week. The guards were continually at us with '*los*', '*arbeit*', '*immer fester*', frequently punctuated with the butt of a rifle. A couple of our men, having been knocked about, reported the matter to a German sergeant-major. His answer was to call up two or three guards and order them to charge.

Early in November the whole place was running alive with vermin. There were no baths, and only two taps on the parade ground for 4,000 men, some 3,000 Russians having joined us. I had a bath in my soup bowl out in the open. The operation was carried out in sections, and it was damned cold. In addition to the lice, a blood rash was coming out in everyone, making it impossible to sleep. Right on until March we remained in this condition, lousy and covered in sores. Some men had scratched themselves raw, and were taken to hospital, where their hands were bandaged and tied up so that they couldn't scratch. The chronic itching nearly drove us crazy.

Another ailment we all suffered from was weak bladders. Our diet was all liquid with the exception of bread, the result being that men would go to the latrines ten or twelve times in one night. The loss of sleep, poor food, and long working days, soon told its tale, and men were fainting at work daily. They were brought back on carts.

On 22 November I had a high temperature and was unable to get up, so I was carried down to the hospital on a stretcher. I still wore the same shirt that I was captured in. I had not had a shave or hair-cut for about two months, so I thought at last I should get cleaned up; but there was nothing doing. I stayed in hospital a week, being medically examined daily. This place was running alive with vermin. I spent most of my time killing them off. I had tonsilitis, but before I was well I was ordered out to make room. I got up straight from bed, and walked back to the camp through snow with a guard. It took me 25 minutes, though it was only ¼ mile from the lager.

While I was in hospital, Matthews, R.F.A., was shot. About 4,000 men were waiting to go through the gate to draw coffee. Those at the back pressed those in front on to the barbed wire. The sentry on the gate ordered the men to get further back. They tried but, owing to the weight behind them, they were unable to move. The guard fired, killing Matthews and wounding three others. Upon returning to the camp I went to the sick tent, but as it leaked worse than my old one, I returned to the latter. I passed the time playing chess (home-made) and bridge, one of the boys having brought some cards with him.

30 November. We moved into huts, similar to those occupied by the German troops, the difference being that we slept on the deck, three men on two mattresses. Each hut had a small lobby. The places were so crowded that some men had to sleep there – in December.

3 December. I heard from home, and wrote my second post

card, asking for money, food, clothes, and tobacco—I had tried tea leaves and oak-apple leaves in my pipe till my tongue was like a piece of leather.

4 December. I had my first haircut and shave, on the Q.T., as no knives or razors were allowed. The 'barber' had found an old knife while loading up rubbish. This he sharpened, and with it shaved several hundred men, most of them getting up with tears in their eyes after the operation.

6 December. The German corporal, generally known as the 'pork butcher', made his appearance. This man was responsible for the greater part of the horrible brutality that took place in Döberitz. He spoke fluent English, and was supposed to have had a butcher's shop in England.

8 December. Holtham of the R.N.D. received a packet of Smith's Glasgow Mixture and gave me a pipeful. Of all the pleasures I have had in my life, this was the greatest.

9 December. My throat was troublesome, so I went to the hospital. Waited outside in snow for three hours. I had my throat painted on the inside with iodine; have you ever experienced this?

12 December. All Roman Catholic Irish left camp. It is not known where they went. We were ordered to move into other huts, half Russians and half English in each hut. This was petty spite on the part of the Germans. We at least tried our best to keep comparatively clean, but the Russians made no attempt. The Russians closed all their windows, so we opened all ours. The Russians complained to the Commandant, who ordered the windows to be closed all night. The place stunk, and the atmosphere was so thick one could hardly see across the room. So several windows were opened to a chorus of howls from the Russkis, of which scant notice was taken.

About 1 am Poole of the R.N.D. was lying awake when a bowlful of ice-cold water was thrown over him, drenching him and his pal. Up they jumped and spotted a Russki skudding across the snow. They noticed a vacant bed on the Russian side, so waited just inside the door. Presently in came a Russian. Bang! right in the mouth. The howls of the Russian woke everyone up, and a general set-to ensued. The amusing part of it was that after quiet had been restored it was found to be the wrong Russian. However, he was easily appeased with a bowlful of soup on the following day, and he became Poole's batman subsequently. The actual perpetrator of the deed was never found.

The 'pork butcher' was in charge of our block, No. 8. His style of punishment for minor offences consisted of tying men to posts on tip-toe with their hands above their heads. After a time the pain was excruciating. The time given was from two to six hours, but with the longer periods the hands were not tied above the heads. Many men fainted on the two-hour spasm. Men who had undergone the punishment have complained to the British authorities. Among them may be mentioned Rudram, Poole and Greenwood of the R.N.D. Rudram, whom I have just visited at Yarmouth, still suffers from the result of being tied up on one leg for 'dodging the column'. He is a North Sea fisherman of a particularly rugged type, and his undying wish is to meet the 'pork butcher' on these shores. He is not the only man holding this wish.

On the last day of 1914 at 9 pm every man was solemnly sitting up in bed 'killing off', which operation was conducted twice daily, morning and night. Scratching was also much in vogue. We told Kirk, the only man with a watch, to call us at 12 pm. This he did and we sang *God Save the King, Rule Britannia, Auld Lang Syne*, and we were just giving the *Marseillaise* and *Hail Columbia*, when a rifle was thrust through the window with the guttural command, '*Ruhig!*'

15 January, 1915. A Russian found selling chocolate in the camp was tied up three hours daily for a week. A Tommy received

the same treatment for stealing some sausage. One working party was told off to sharpen bayonets; they refused.

Parcels from England were now making their appearance, and camp life improved immensely in consequence. Men began to repair their clothes and smarten up generally. Football was played on the square, and cards in the evening, while the 'Crown and Anchor' boards were attracting their usual numbers. Pontoon was the favourite card game; brag, nap and solo were good seconds, only a few indulging in bridge.

Smoking in the huts was '*strong verboten*'. How that word riled us. Everything was *verboten* at one time or another, except work, and there was always bags of that. Needless to say, we always did smoke in the huts, the unfortunates who were caught being tied up.

7 May. Captain A., second-in-command, gave orders to posterns to instil discipline into British prisoners of war with rifle butts, bayonets to be used if necessary. Printed notices to this effect were posted up in the barracks. In fact the death sentence appeared applicable to any crime from 'pinching spuds' to 'dodging the column'.

In the German barracks '*Gott strafe England*' was chalked up in many conspicuous places. It was also the headline on their bread coupon cards. On one occasion a party of 20 British were returning from work. They met a company of Germans, whose officer commanded our party to halt and face his company. When we were in position, and wondering what was coming next, he rode up to our party and shouted '*Gott strafe England*', these words being repeated by his whole company. Then with a look as if he had just stormed a position, he marched his company off, and German *kultur* scored another victory.

12 May. Russian killed and ate a German NCO's white cat. He received three days' cells. The next morning, as the Russians filed on parade, our boys greeted them with cat-calls, causing a

good deal of amusement. A German NCO, known as Tubby, rushed up to us demanding silence and the cause of the outburst. When he was told, '*Militarismus*' went by the way, and he was convulsed with mirth. (It was not his cat.) This was the first occasion upon which I had heard a German laugh on parade.

13 May. Ascension day, and a holiday. Every man in camp paraded at 8 am. In the middle of the parade ground, facing us, two Russians were tied up with their hands above their heads. They had attempted to escape, but were recaptured, and this was the punishment, five hours daily. Both men were moaning. One of them fainted while we were still on parade, and the other man was only just conscious.

Our men signified their disapproval by shouting at the Germans to untie them. While this uproar was going on, a Russian sergeant-major went up and complained to a German NCO. The Russian was promptly kicked and ordered back to the ranks. He refused to go. Guards were called up and he was arrested. The whole parade was then ordered to barracks, the order being accompanied by a couple of shots.

When we were inside, German interpreters came round saying, 'The guards have orders to shoot on sight any man on parade or looking through windows.' This was 11 o'clock in the morning, and indiscriminate firing was carried on till 4 pm. Three Russians were killed and several wounded. Most of the huts in our block had bullet holes through them.

1 June. Another hell of a day. Breakfast 5 am. Four-mile walk. Carrying trees for four hours. Got back at 2 pm. Had to turn out in afternoon, carrying iron bedsteads from station till 6 pm.

2 June. Hot day; cleaning out deep ditch, stunk like blazes, working in water. Received splendid parcel. Sausages top hole.

Cricket in the evening was very popular, and Army and Navy matches created a great deal of interest, a couple of thousand men looking on. We got the shoe-mender to cover tennis balls with leather, making a very good ball. A hard ball was too dangerous under the confined conditions. We purchased some matting from Berlin as the parade ground was too sandy to permit of a good pitch. The elevens representing the different regiments possessed some good talent, and the game was played strictly to rules. Many keen contests took place, promoting good fellowship through the camp.

3 August. McDonald of the R.N.D. killed. We had been to fetch sand from the plains, and coming back McDonald and another were on the pole of the first wagon. They came to a sharp dip. The heavy wagon got out of control. McDonald fell, and the wheel passed over him, killing him. There were no brakes on the wagon.

6 August. Scotty, another Britisher, shot. His mind became affected on 13 May, when the shooting affair took place. He was taken to hospital, escaped from there, wandered to the lager, and tried to scale the barbed wire. The sentry killed him.

7 August. All privileges to British prisoners of war stopped. The reason given was the alleged brutal treatment by the British Government of German civilians interned in England. This meant no sports, no cards, and all musical instruments were taken from us.

Life from now on was pretty miserable. Some more new guards made their appearance, and one in particular was a holy terror. He and another took ten men to Spandau, shovelling clinker. Before the men started, he told them he had seen his own brother bayonetted on the west front by an Englishman. If ever a man hated Englishmen it was this fellow. He was over 6 ft in height. If a man stopped working, he got a blow from the butt end from him.

The men used to return to camp with their hands blistered and bleeding. Complaints were made to the *kommandant*, so a different ten were sent daily. I went on that fatigue once. I shovelled coke with a coke shovel for eight hours, and didn't stop working once. I was all in when I finished, and by the time I got back to the lager at 8 pm I was just boiling over with resentment.

On 27 August Farrant was lucky enough to be allocated a 'cushy number', and for the next six months his life 'ran along in pleasant channels'. With three other men he was deputed to assist a Berlin artist in the decoration of a new Roman Catholic Church that had been built and presented to the German troops quartered in Döberitz by Graf von Spee, brother of the late Admiral von Spee. The work involved nothing more arduous than rigging scaffolding, sand-papering window frames and painting in stencilled patterns of flowers and angels on the semi-circular roof.

Hard frosts in November and December, with the temperature falling to 20 degrees below zero, added appreciably to the hospital queues, but at the same time gave impetus to plans for celebrating Christmas in festive style.

Christmas Day, 1915—a day that will long linger in the memory of the Döberitz prisoners of war. Having by this time become familiar with the country, arrangements had for some time been made with German civvies to supply liquor. The boys determined to celebrate this Christmas, and some thousands of bottles of schnapps and other stuff were smuggled into the camp.

The fun started on Christmas Eve. We made a collection of grub and handed it over to the Russians. A Russian doctor, who was employed at the hospital, visited our barracks to thank us on behalf of the Russians. He had just finished a speech in our hut, and a good deal of cheering ensued, when in bounced a German officer and two guards. The officer demanded lights out immediately. This was at 9 o'clock. We had made a request for lights until 10 pm, which was granted by the commandant.

Petty Officer M., who was in charge of the hut, and who was half-seas-over, told the officer to clear out as he was in charge and wasn't going to be interfered with by any damned German. He then laid hands on the officer. The two guards made a rush and M. was pulled back by some of the boys just in time. The officer and the two guards went out and up to the guard-house and turned out the guard. There was an ominous sound of clicking magazines, and the party marched towards our barracks. Half-way across they were stopped by the deputy officer in charge of the lager. Thus another shooting spasm was nipped in the bud. The officer of the guard exceeded his duty by coming into the lager without permission of the acting commandant. M. received 14 days; he was lucky.

The next day hardly a man was sober. It didn't take long to make a man 'see red' on this stuff, commonly called 'fixed bayonets'. Plenty of scraps took place, old grievances were aired, challenges to fight any man in the place were issued by men of all sizes. In fact it was difficult to walk down the room without getting tangled up with someone. It was a gay old time.

The whole camp was placed under punishment for a month in consequence of this celebration by General von A., who inspected the camp shortly after this affair. No sports or recreation; every man to be in bed at 7 pm: no lights and no talking: the guards were ordered to fire at any light in the barracks seen after 7 pm. We were jolly glad when the month was up.

The first successful escape from Döberitz recorded by Farrant had taken place in November, when a Royal Naval Division man named Miller had managed to reach Denmark. (Farrant notes that he later received a commission in the RAF and was killed in 1917.) Escape had evidently been in Farrant's mind for some time. He was not even put off by a spell in the camp hospital in March, 1916, at a time when 'a man had to be practically down and out before he received medical attention'. In April, with three other men (Kirkaldy, Reinert and Rumbelow), a plot was hatched to escape in civilian clothes and travel by train to the Dutch border during the Easter holiday week-end.

Civilian clothes were smuggled from a large consignment in the camp stores that had been sent from England. A guard was bribed to obtain a train time-table. To the 300 marks the four men had between them, a navy stoker, renowned in the camp as a gambler, generously added a further 350 marks in silver, saying to Farrant, 'It's in a good cause, Towny—hope you get through.'

On the night of Thursday, 20 April, the four men managed to cut through the two lines of barbed wire that surrounded the camp undetected, at a point where Rumbelow, who was the lager electrician, had disconnected one of the electric lights.

All four made our way to the road as quickly as possible as we had lost valuable time. We had a mile and a half to walk to the station. Rumbelow was just purchasing two tickets and we could hear the train coming in when Reinert came rushing up, and in his excitement shouted out in English, 'Get four, you damn fool', following this up with '*Noch zwei bitte!*' Fortunately no one seemed to have noticed the foreign language, but we missed the train by seconds. There was nothing for it but to hang about and catch the next train in an hour's time.

We caught this and reached Spandau, a suburb of Berlin, about 10.15 pm. We walked up and down the streets of Spandau for two and a half hours, splitting up into pairs. I was carrying a week's provisions for the four of us, and well I knew it by the time our train came in. Reinert bought the tickets and we were just going through the barrier when the booking clerk tapped on the window. We all thought the game was up, but Reinert had left the change on the counter and the booking clerk had merely knocked to attract his attention. Gad! We were relieved.

We passed through the guards at the barrier, and had not long to wait for the train. It was full up with German soldiers. We tried to get in, but were told only military were allowed in. Just as the train was moving off and we were about to be left, a porter opened the door of a carriage without any light and in we jumped.

We repassed our lager with the gap between the lights showing quite plainly, and hoped we should never see it again.

About 3 am we had to change carriages. We got in a second class, in which two German soldiers and two civvies were seated. As soon as it was light, conversation was started by the soldier on my left. What he didn't say about England wouldn't be worth writing, his remarks being endorsed by the other Jerries. Rumbelow spoke once or twice; so to keep up appearances I asked him if he knew the time, in German. In trying to speak in an off-hand manner I made a most horrible jargon of it by using the verb '*kennen*' instead of '*wissen*'. The civvy opposite me cast an inquiring glance in my direction, and as I didn't speak any more he kept his eyes on me for the rest of the journey. I felt every minute he was going to question me. I was jolly glad when we reached Hanover at 6 o'clock in the morning.

As we had missed the fast train, we found that we must change at Hanover, so Reinert asked the time that the Reine train left and also the platform. And then we made a fatal mistake. The train for Reine was not due for an hour, and instead of waiting in the station restaurant, we went up on to the platform, where we looked conspicuous in our shabby clothes and dirty boots.

On the platform besides ourselves were a German officer and a station official and two or three porters. As we were walking up and down in pairs, I noticed the officer nod in our direction and speak to the official. Both of them approached us and, saluting, asked where we were going. We told them. 'What are you?' 'Electricians from Berlin going for a holiday.' 'Kindly produce your passports.' As we could not produce them we were arrested. Reinert tried the official with a hundred mark note, but he merely shrugged his shoulders and said, '*Ich darf nicht.*'

We were handed over to the police and subsequently to the military authorities, and put in a small room with three armed guards to await the OC. At last he came and, after giving in our names, he asked if we were hungry. We replied in the affirmative. Then he said, 'Have you any money?' We replied, 'Plenty'. To our utter astonishment this remarkable German said he would arrange for some food. Would we have expensive food or cheap food. We replied, 'The best in town.' Kirkaldy followed this up with a request for beer, which, however, was not granted.

For the next ten minutes we could discuss nothing else than this unparalleled instance of a German officer showing courtesy to British prisoners of war. We had a topping feed and spent the afternoon waving our hands and giving the glad eye to the girls as they passed our window, which was on a level with the street. Little did they know we were Britishers.

At midnight three guards from Döberitz turned up. They were three beauties. They searched us for arms and knives, and told us they would shoot us at the slightest provocation. We were escorted to the train. As soon as the crowd heard we were escaped British prisoners of war, they became hostile and crowded round the carriage, shaking their fists and cursing us generally.

We reached Döberitz the next morning. The big Easter sports programme arranged for Friday, Saturday and Sunday, had been stopped as they found we had left the camp half an hour after we had gone. Search parties had been sent out in many directions, but they never thought of the station. We gave in particulars as to how we got our clothes etc, but we had rehearsed this coming down the line, so none of the boys who helped us got into trouble.

We were stripped and put into prison garb and given clogs, then banged into cells to await our sentence. We were five days on bread and water awaiting sentence, which was fourteen days 'strong arrest'. This meant bread and water, soup every fourth day, pitch dark cells, and no exercise. And this is where our bid for liberty landed us.

In May, 1916, Farrant was in a party of 1,000 PoWs transferred to

Russia. His experiences during much of the next eighteen months, apart from a few 'cushy' periods, make even Döberitz sound tolerable. Camp locations ranged from mosquito-infested swamps to the German front line trenches, where the British PoWs were equally at the mercy of snow blizzard and Allied shells. The working week was never less than 6½ days.

On 14 May the party disentrained at Zeren, south-west of the Gulf of Riga. Next day, after a nightmare twelve-hour march through forest and swamps, they reached the village of Kilizeem. While the rest of the party entrained here for another destination, Farrant found himself in a company of 100 PoWs quartered in a farm at the end of the village.

This place had barbed wire round it, and was merely a collection of cowsheds and barns. The cowshed that I was detailed to was in use as a temporary hospital. There was about a foot of cow dung and straw on the floor, over which some fresh straw had been strewn. As soon as the *sanitäts** cleared out, we 'mucked out' till we came to solid earth. We then secured some planks, and rigged up a shelf on which to sleep. Our place was the best in the lager.

There was not room enough for everybody in the sheds, and some of the boys built themselves 'kennels', made by laying spits of turf one on another, and using old boards with straw laid on top for a roof. The water in the wells stunk, and we were warned not to use it. When boiled it was a dark yellow colour, but it was the only water available.

22 May. The first day's work nearly ended in a riot. The men refused to work; guards threatened two prisoners with the bayonet, but they wouldn't budge. The prisoners were knocked down twice with rifles, but still refused. The rest of the men showed signs of settling the guards, so the guards brought the party back in lager. Paraded for two hours; general hell. No parcel, no tobacco, and damned hungry.

* Medical Orderly.

23 May. The guards were reinforced and the men worked 11 hours felling trees. The mosquitoes were unbearable. Forty men reported sick, but the doctor sent every man to work without inspecting anyone. The guards used their butt ends frequently. Our NCO in charge told the German officer that if this brutality continued there would be a mutiny.

25 May. About 25 men refused to leave the camp and were stood up all day until 6 pm with nothing to eat.

26 May. A new officer, Lt. G., made his appearance to take over. He started shouting as soon as he came on parade, and this precipitated matters. Those at the gate had just marched off, but the rest refused to move. The officer telephoned for a squad of Uhlans.* They arrived about 11 am, with an active service officer in charge. He ordered the Uhlans to line up in the front of the men, load their carbines, and then made the following announcement, which was interpreted:

'You have been sent to Russia as a reprisal. Your Government has handed over to the French 2,000 of our soldiers, many of whom are professional men. They are made to work on the docks, and while they are so employed you will be kept here in Russia and made to work. I will give you one minute to decide, and then I shall order my men to fire.'

This resulted in the majority deciding to work, but some eight still refused. These men were taken by the Uhlans to some trees outside the lager and tied up, the Uhlans banging them in their faces with their fists. The next day defaulters were also tied up, and then taken to work, the Uhlans knocking the men about all day.

28 May. This was Sunday. Uhlans turned every man out at 4.30 am. After a cup of coffee the men were marched to the forest where we were employed felling trees. At night, after coffee was served, the whole camp was put through a saluting parade,

* German Cavalry.

all this on two cups of coffee and three slices of bread, ¾" thick. The soup served at midday was nothing but a drink. The Uhlans left next day.

Until parcels arrived, nettles, oats and wheat were boiled and eaten. A few sheaves of corn were found in a barn. The ears were broken off and were put in a handkerchief, and beaten on a stone to liberate the grains. A good deal of stomach trouble was caused through eating partly boiled oats, but it was a case of 'What won't fatten will fill'. The mosquitoes in this place gave us no rest day or night. It was a case of either sleeping with one's head under a blanket or walking about the lager most of the night.

4 June. Every man was inoculated. Quite a number of men went down and out after the operation. We were all very weak owing to insufficient nourishment.

6 June. Some parcels arrived. A week later the German rations were cut down by 25%. A note to the American Ambassador was written by our NCOs complaining about our rations being reduced. This did not get past the officer, who, however, promised us the full amount of rations allowed.

8 July. Sentry struck one of our men, who struck him back. The Englishman was taken to the guard's house, being manhandled on the way, and put in cells; he got 12 months' imprisonment subsequently.

9 July. Several men who had committed offences in Germany and who had been sent to Russia before their term of punishment was finished, were, by an order from their lager *kommandant*, to complete their punishment here. It was unfortunate that this order should have come after the striking incident of yesterday as the following will show.

Six men were taken to the forest just outside the lager and were made to stand on blocks of wood with their backs to the trees, to which they were then lashed and the blocks kicked away. In one case a man (McQuitty of the Canadians) was suspended by his arms. He and a soldier named Mason made sworn statements concerning their treatment. These statements were taken down by one of our NCOs and handed in to the officer commanding, who replied that the matter would be inquired into. Mason, who fainted after he was untied, had been previously excused all work by the German doctor as he was physically unfit. The guards who tied the men up in this fashion told them it was on account of one of our men striking a guard.

After two months at Kilizeem Farrant was on the move again. During his eighteen months in Russia he was quartered in six different camps, for periods ranging from two to five months. Not knowing what was to happen next, whether the next camp would be more or less endurable, above all whether the all-important food parcels from home would be available, must at least have kept hope flickering throughout the ordeal.

The four months after Kilizeem were, indeed, what Farrant describes as 'a very good number'. August and September of 1916 he spent, with five other PoWs, sorting letters and parcels at a *kommandos*' headquarters at Stenden. During October and November he was engaged on similar light duty at Hasenporth, some 40 miles from the port of Libau. Later he was to return to Libau to work at the docks. It was back-breaking work but, as Farrant now discovered, there was a very special reason that made this treadmill one that every prisoner was happy to endure.

Arriving at Libau on 3 October, four of us, with a German guard, went up to the English lager where the other party of 1,000 Englishmen had been sent from Döberitz. On our way up we passed a company of about 200 of our men swinging down the road in great style. It was a good sight, and German soldiers and Russian civilians stopped to see them go by. Every man was spick and span, cap badges and buttons shone like silver, all 'chucking a chest' and marching in step. These 'Old Contemptibles' made a fine advertisement for the British Empire.

It didn't take us long to find the reason for this extra smart appearance. These men were working at the docks, and so were some 2,000 Lettish girls. When our boys first made their appearance in Libau in May, the girls working on the docks dressed mostly in sacks and wooden clogs, and were known by the men as 'donkeys', as they were employed generally in pulling carts about. But it was not very long before each sex started smartening up in appearance. The 'donkeys' now wore shoes and stockings with generally a very English-looking red handkerchief tied round their heads, while they had discarded sacks for something smarter.

Conversation was '*strong verboten*' between the Lettish girls and our men. It can be imagined how much effect that order had. Each man more or less had his special 'donkey', and used to take her chocolate when he got it in his parcel, and she in return would occasionally half-hitch a bottle of rum for him.

It was hard work on the docks, but I never knew a party that wanted to leave Libau and the 'donkeys'. The work of our men consisted of loading and unloading provisions. Carrying a 240-lb sack on one's back from the ship's side into the store and up four flights of steps, seven hours daily, is no child's play, and several men became ruptured by slipping with this weight on their backs.

It goes without saying that men at Libau were seldom hungry, though parties were searched at the docks, and again in the lager. Secreting foodstuff became an art, at which the Lettish girls were not far behind our men. Their favourite ruse was to dampen the flour and make a thick paste and lay a good sized cake on either shoulder under their blouses. It really was amusing to see our men unload when they were out of sight of the guards; slabs of raw meat, and small bags of flour and sugar were hauled out from most uncanny places. Sergeant Pinchen of the Manchesters afforded the best laugh when asked if he had 'got away' with anything. His answer was to take off his woollen scarf, which was twisted round his neck, and throw it on the table. There before our gaze lay a string of twelve prime sausages which had been enfolded in his scarf.

During the first two months of 1917 Farrant was quartered in an overcrowded brick schoolhouse at a town called Erbsen Krug, 60 miles from the comparative fleshpots of Libau. In freezing conditions, his 6½-day working week was spent levelling ground for a light railway. But worse was to come—the worst, surely, that any prisoners of the Germans in World War I had to endure. On 25 February, in company with 100 Royal Naval Division men, he disentrained at Ekau, to be marched 17 kilometres in a blizzard to a place called Reiskatte. They were at the Russian front.

We entered a barbed wire enclosure in which were two or three dugouts. Over the gate a sign bore the words '*Vergeltung Lager*' (Reprisal Camp). We were kept on parade for 2½ hours in the snow. New numbers were given us and our kits searched. We were then told to go into the dugouts, and as usual we were overcrowded.

26 February. We paraded at 6 am. The lieutenant in charge announced through an interpreter that we 100 men would be sent daily into the trenches to work, as German prisoners of war were employed by the British in their trenches. While they continued to keep German prisoners under shell fire, so long should we be kept here. Further a man or men would be shot upon the slightest provocation. We were then told to write home and state that we were in the German firing line. The lager was about 5 kilometres from the first line.

We were then split into two groups of 40 and 60. The 60 party, which was the dayshift, left the lager at 6.15 am. Our party of 40 left at 4 pm and met the others returning, who said that they had been under fire most of the day but no casualties. We arrived at the third line at 6 pm where we were given shovels. A lieutenant addressed our guards, telling them we were on no account to cease working, and rubbing in that the German prisoners were receiving brutal treatment in the British lines.

The first night's work consisted of shovelling snow out of the third line, which was completely filled. The first lines of German trenches were, in this section, from 50 to 300 yards from the Russian lines. The second German trench was 200 yards from the first, and the third trench 200 yards from the second. The place had once been a forest, but shell fire had swept it clean.

We returned to the lager at 3 am, tired out. We had been away from the lager for 11 hours. The Germans weren't content with this, for the next morning the night party had to do an hour's camp fatigue from 10 to 11 am.

1 March. At Point 111/35, 50 yards from the first line, 150 yards from the Russian line, pulling sleighs loaded with timbers, frequently had to take shelter from machine-gun fire. German soldiers in trenches bore us no malice, and were surprised that we should be working here.

2 March. Our party carrying 'bird cages', weighing about 300lb, two men to a 'birdcage', having to carry them 1 kilometre, usually done with five rests. They cut our shoulders, and it was the most straining work I have ever done. These bird cages, as we call them, were about 18′ long, and consisted of a 4″ pole with wooden crosses at each end and one in the centre, round which barbed wire was wound. They were about 5′ high and were used to repair the barbed wire entanglement. We walked 25 kilometres between 4 pm and 2.30 am, carrying from 6 pm till 1 am. We had to keep moving to prevent frostbite, but my finger was bitten in spite of that.

3 March. Below zero. We were in the second line, and we were stamping our feet for six solid hours. The ground was like iron. We couldn't work. We were supposed to trim off corners and level

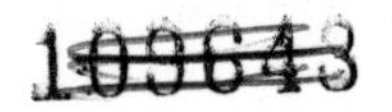
109643

the bottom. The guards were dancing up and down as well. They were relieved every two hours. A Russian machine gunner had located us, so we had to keep our heads down.

5 March. Day shift. Called 5.15 am. Coffee (for want of a better name as it was made from burnt barley and other stuff) 5.45. Fell in 6.15. Trenches at 8 am. Four of us were digging a hole for a rubbish shoot. The picks were blunt, and we didn't pick two barrowfuls all day. Scott, one of our party, was cursing the cold and things in general with vehement bitterness, when his pick fell out of his hands and down he went in exhaustion. I went over to him but he was motionless. I asked the guard to let us take him into a dugout. He merely shrugged and said, '*Es geht nicht*'. While I was expostulating with the guard, a German NCO came up and he allowed us to take Scott into a dugout where he thawed out. He was helped back to the lager when we returned.

Just after we had taken Scott in, our little party was subjected to about 20 rounds. They were bursting unpleasantly close. The guard was all right, in the lee of a substantial dugout, but wouldn't let us get shelter until the same NCO came out of a dugout and ordered the guard to take us to an '*Unterstand*', a specially constructed shelter, until the firing was over.

7 March. We were searched for diaries and some were found. We were now beginning to feel the effect of insufficient nourishment as all the food we had brought with us had been eaten. We were strictly on German rations, which were 2/5ths of a 3-lb loaf per day per man. This was the only solid food we had. Coffee substitute was served at 5.30 am, and soup at night. What soup it was! consisting of dried vegetable or pigeon peas, or horse beans. The amount of solids in the soup never amounted to more than two or three spoonsful. Twice a week we were supposed to have meat. The meat was boiled in the copper, but before we drew our soup the solid meat was fished out and divided among the

guards. The same graft was carried out with the jam, a large portion being scooped out from our issue for the guards. We never had potatoes.

11 March. Sunday. We had all looked forward to this day of rest, and to mend and wash our things, but we were disappointed. We were called at 5 am and were kept shovelling snow till 11 am, returned to lager for soup at 4 pm. We were marched to trenches and worked till 2 am, returning to lager at 3.30 am, badly done up. One man collapsed. It was the coldest night yet, 10 degrees Fahrenheit below zero. From my knees down my legs were numb for 11 hours. We had been working for nearly 20 hours.

12 March. On account of an alleged entry made in C's diary to the effect that we were working sixteen hours a day, the actual working hours were extended as a punishment for recording incorrect statements. The guards were lectured and their attitude to us from now on was distinctly hostile, as they had to participate in the longer period.

The actual time in the trenches was from 6 pm till 2 am. No matter if the work was finished or not, one hour pause was allowed. By orders issued we were not allowed in the German dugouts, and to stand in the trenches for an hour without working meant getting frostbitten. Indeed to prevent this we worked straight on, but the damned swine wouldn't allow us to leave an hour earlier. So while this bitter weather continued we worked an extra hour. The guards were doing an hour on and an hour off, going to warm dugouts for their stand easy. We were all weak from hunger and long hours, and men used to stumble and sway about every night when returning to the lager, often turning in without undressing. One or two men had watches, and every few minutes someone or other would ask the time. I was glad I had no watch.

14 March. Returned to lager 4 am, coughed continuously till 7 am; got up at 8 am and saw doctor, who gave me some tablets

and ordered me to work; turned in from 10 am till 2 pm. Started for another night shift at 4 pm; came back to lager 12 hours later absolutely knocked.

17 March. The most bitter night I have ever experienced. Men complained about thinness of soup. The Lieutenant went into a rage, and told us we were getting all we were allowed.

18 March. Sunday. Reached lager exhausted. Temperature below zero and blizzard part of the day. Couldn't keep warm, although we had a fire in our dugout.

19 March. Paraded 7 am, clearing snow till 8 am, then marched for two hours in deep snow to new position. Worked till 4 pm with no stand easy, two hours walk back. Done up, drank soup, and turned in.

I don't know how much longer I can stick it; my strength has just about given out, but I can still smoke.

20 March. Felling trees in 2′ of snow. Swapped some soap for bread with German soldier. We carried on with this work for a week, and of all the Germans I have met there is one who stands out as a white man; he is the NCO in charge of the wood party. He offered us the remainder of his soup which was brought out to him daily. At this time I was physically incapable of using an axe for felling, but I could use the saw which was much easier.

The veneer of civilization was wearing off rapidly. Men seldom spoke; when they did, it was always about food. A man was exchanging a piece of soap for a piece of bread one day, but another fellow pulled out a larger piece of soap and walked up to the German and got the bread. The second man was 'birded' by the party, but little he cared; it was every man for himself. '*Dieu et mon Droit*', which translated into navy speech is 'To hell with you Jack, I'm all right,' was practised on all sides.

30 March. Our party on returning to lager were searched again for diaries. While we were at work the Germans had gone

through our kit bags. My diaries were in the toe of my sleeping bag, and it was on this occasion I almost decided to destroy my notes, as some of the men had been knocked about all day owing to C's diary being found, and naturally our own men were pretty sore. 25% sick, mostly of frostbite and general weakness.

2 April. My birthday. I celebrated it by having an extra slice of bread, which meant this much less for next day. The bread ration yielded 5 thin slices about ½″ thick by 4″ square. The division of the ration was a matter of vital interest. There is only one fair way, and it is this: the loaf is cut into portions, every man taking an eager interest in the cutting. Then one man turns his back, and as the cutter indicates a certain portion, the man with his back to the bread calls out a man's name, the man named taking the portion indicated, and so on.

We were officially informed on parade that we should receive no parcels at all while we were here. The result of this news was rather unexpected, inasmuch as there was less 'cribbing'. Men felt that they had got down to bedrock and couldn't get any further, and that the only thing to do was to stick it.

5 April. Two men dropped at work.

6 April. Four men dropped at work and were taken back to lager.

10 April. Men swapping underclothes and jerseys for bread. Some rotten fish was thrown out from the German cook house. Some of the men ate it, and were violently sick later. Occasionally soup bones, which had been boiled up in the cooker for the German, were thrown out. They were bare of meat, but we used to boil them over again and drink the water, crack the bones, eat the marrow, and chew the spongy portions of the bones.

15 April. We were disinfected. It was when we were in the bath house (in the German quarters) that men realized the privations they had suffered. We were like skeletons; shoulder bones, hip bones, knees and elbows were horribly prominent.

17 April. Received letters from home; the first for two months. We were paraded and informed that France had withdrawn the German prisoners of war from the firing line, but that England had not.

20 April. Parcels arrived. The next day each man received a parcel after returning from work. The parcels were then deposited on the parade ground for inspection. The German Lieutenant ordered men to open tins in order to view the contents. No one slept that night, the excitement was too great. Some ate half the contents of their parcel the same night. Many were up at 3 am cooking burgoo for breakfast.

22 April. Sunday, no work and a lovely day. Today each man drew tobacco or cigarettes. Men said 'Good morning' to each other. Some even whistled and sung, the first exhibition of pleasure that had ever taken place in this cursed spot. This was the happiest day I ever spent as a prisoner of war. We were men again. It was great, and all on account of a little extra food.

3 May. Bread ration reduced to three slices. Young of the R.N.D. died. He had been excused duty, but not admitted to hospital. He died in the dugout.

The cold weather was now breaking up, snowing and fine alternately. Heavy artillery became more active on both sides. At the end of May, before the snow had melted, the mosquitoes became very bad, for we were right in the swamps which lie south-west of Riga.

10 June. Received orders to move. The reprisal was over.

Walking skeletons, the reprisal victims were returned to Libau. There Farrant met some of another group of 500 men who had been through the same ordeal in the German trenches. Several men of this company, he was told, had died from starvation and cold.

After a week's rest, Farrant's company was put to work on the docks.

It was a six and a half days' working week, but with football on Sunday afternoons and the inestimable bonus of the Lettish 'donkeys'. With the latter Farrant appears to have been only obliquely involved.

Each man more or less had his special 'donkey', whom he saw at the docks every day. The hurried scraps of daily conversation were in many cases supplemented by letters written in German at night and exchanged the following day. Some men wrote their own love letters, while others obtained the assistance of those who could 'speak the bat'. My services were occasionally requisitioned.

On one occasion a big North Sea fisherman from Stornoway told me his 'donkey' wouldn't speak to him because she had seen him yarning with another girl, and would I write a letter for him. So I told him to leave it to me. It took two hours to write that letter and I handed it to him the same night. Being Scotch, he wanted me to translate it to him, so I read him the more prosaic passages and away he went. If that 'donkey', upon reading the letter didn't think she was the best looking girl in Kurland then it was because the dictionary I used wasn't big enough. The next night Mac said 'It's alright', so I asked him if he had any chocolate to spare: he just grinned.

Farrant's account of his last sixteen months as a prisoner of war is a good deal shorter than in the earlier periods and there are few personal references. At Libau he was taken off humping sacks after six weeks and employed in 'writing signs'. Early in December, 1917, he left Russia for Chemnitz in Saxony, where he was to spend the rest of the war. Initially he was lucky enough to get a clerical job, but it is not clear whether he was later drafted to one of the *kommandos* employed at factories, farms and road works. What he was spared was the 'hell' of the coal mines.

Chemnitz had about 20,000 PoWs on its books, of many nationalities, housed in barracks converted from stables. Discipline was severe.

0429509

A sports field where Sunday football was played was also used for punishment. Defaulters were drilled in squads, each man carrying an old German pack, filled with stones and weighing about 60lb. Punishment drill lasted two hours, and consisted of running, halting, lying down, getting up and running again. Many a man collapsed under it. One German sergeant-major in particular 'had it in' for the Britishers. He was called 'Willie Woodbine' because he was thin and anaemic.

The worst punishment of all was to be put to work in the coal mines. Condemned mines at Oelsnitz had been reopened and British prisoners of war were compelled to go below. They worked absolutely naked. At first men wore their boots, but the sweat made this impossible, and soon everyone went bare-footed. There was a night shift and a day shift. The men slept in crowded quarters and had no recreation. Indeed, they were only too glad to turn in after a meal.

The place was alive with fleas and bugs, and continued in this condition the whole of the time our men were there. In eight months 65% of the original number were returned to lager as unfit for work, and a man had to be very bad before he was excused duty. No two Englishmen were allowed to work together. As a rule a gang consisted of three Germans and one Englishman. There were numerous cases of manhandling. Self-inflicted wounds, like slashing arms and legs and rubbing in dirt to induce blood poisoning, were not infrequent. Anything to get away from that hell on earth, Oeslnitz.

In May, 1918, one of the R.N.D. men was sent back from the mines suffering from brain trouble. He was quite off his head. The poor devil would implore every one he met to stop him from being sent to the mines again. Later another man, belonging to the R.F.A., was brought back in a similar condition. He was subsequently sent to an insane asylum. He would wake up in the middle of the night with a yell that startled the whole barrack-room, mentioning many times the name of 'Knock-out Brown', a German NCO, whose name was K—, one of the worst type of man-handling bullies we had met. He was reported and court-martialled, but never received any punishment as far as we knew.

By the end of October, 1918, the news from the Western Front had the camp at Chemnitz on its toes with excitement. Maps were brought out from hiding places and the Allies' advancing line was marked daily. On 9 November, the day that revolution against the Kaiser and his war lords swept Germany and a republic was proclaimed in Berlin, Farrant recorded a sight he had never thought to see.

German officers coming into the lager to carry on their duties were not saluted by the German sentries. In one case I distinctly saw a German sentry wait until the officer was within three paces of him, and then deliberately turn about so that his back was toward the officer. As soon as he had passed he turned round to his former position. The iron discipline had snapped.

It was another six weeks before Farrant, now suffering from abscesses on his legs and an arm, boarded a British warship at Copenhagen in company with other men of the Royal Naval Division, gaunt shadows of their pre-war selves. His last four diary entries tersely complete his story.

17 December. Sighted lightship on Scottish coast at 6.30 pm.

18 December. Landed at Leith, where we had a top hole reception. Entrained at 4.30 pm. Arrived at Ripon 11 pm. We filled out papers and gave in the names of Germans who had been guilty of brutal treatment to prisoners.

20 December. Medical inspection, rekitted, money changed, and each man received rail warrant and money.

21 December. Entrained 11 am, reached London 8 pm, and home at 10 pm. The excitement kept me going the first night, but

on the next I was delirious, and was kept in bed for a week or two as the result of blood poisoning.

From the recollections of John Farrant, his son, and of Charles Burton, his business colleague from 1912 until his retirement, Farrant emerges as a man physically and mentally equipped to survive his harrowing experiences without lasting effects.

Before the war he had received his early training as a mining engineer in the primitive mining settlements of Colorado and elsewhere in the United States, where conditions were rough and tough enough to prepare him for all but the worst of the German PoW camps. All his life he was physically tough, at one time surviving an operation for cancer, successfully betting the surgeon that he would beat him at golf within a time far shorter than medical opinion deemed possible.

Temperamentally he could be seen as taking after his aunt, Margaret Bondfield, who fought her way in the Labour movement to become Britain's first woman Cabinet Minister. Work was Farrant's ruling passion, and after the war he rose rapidly to become recognized as one of Europe's leading mining engineers.

During the Second World War, as a major in the Home Guard, he channelled his expertise into the construction of fortifications and tunnels, ('fighting Hitler and the A.R.P. boffins with equal zest,' comments John Farrant). Even after his retirement he kept in touch with his old firm in an advisory capacity and lectured on technical matters to the Imperial College, though allowing himself more leisure for his two hobbies, golf and lawn cultivation, in both of which he excelled.

Charles Burton remembers him as 'all hard muscle and drive, married to his job, a firm disciplinarian with his staff, a man who didn't suffer fools gladly, but who could reveal an engaging sense of humour.'

It is the sense of humour that John Farrant chiefly recalls. 'He was no disciplinarian so far as my sister and I were concerned. He was great fun to be with and a wonderful father. Concerning his experiences as a prisoner of war he was very reticent, but I do remember him saying that on occasions the prisoners were so hungry that they chewed up their leather belts.'

After all the brutalities he had experienced or witnessed, Farrant could not entirely forgive and forget. 'My father did not bear ill-will to the Germans as a nation,' says John Farrant. 'But he had an undying hatred for individual Germans. After reading his diary account for the first time, I find that scarcely surprising.'

Chapter Two

DODGING THE COLUMN

LEADING SEAMAN ERIC SURREY DANE

'A DISLIKE OF work is inborn in every average Serviceman and is just as much part of his kit as his tunic. But with prisoners of war this dislike, backed by the very acceptable theory that all work done for the Boche was an unpatriotic act as it released labour to be used against our Forces, developed into a highly specialized art.'

'Dodging the column', as described by Eric Surrey Dane, was an art in which he himself became a past master. His account of how for nine months he evaded the treadmill of working parties by acting as an interpreter, though possessing only the most rudimentary knowledge of the German language, is a highlight of his unfinished journal. The battle of wits against camp officers and guards, that did much to counter the humiliation and enliven the drudgery of life behind barbed wire, is a recurrent theme in PoW accounts (though rarely alluded to by Farrant). With Surrey Dane it was a game to be played with relish. It was no surprise to learn from his late brother, William Surrey Dane, that as a boy he was 'always mischievous and up to pranks'.

Surrey Dane's handwritten manuscript is a jumble of half-completed chapters and fragmentary notes, mostly relating to the earlier periods of his captivity. But there is enough to indicate that he shared many of the hardships and brutalities described by Farrant, including those terrible three-and-a-half months in the German trenches. What makes comparison of their two accounts of particular interest are the very different impressions of camp life that they give. Temperament is a factor that must always be taken into account in reading of the experiences of PoWs.

Even making allowances for the fact that Surrey Dane was writing from memory, and that he was little more than a boy at the time of his capture, his account is altogether more light-hearted than that of the older and maturer Farrant. It is like looking through two ends of the telescope at the same scene: Farrant's the distant, detached view, Surrey Dane's the close-up, lively with detail, involved.

In what would doubtless have been the second chapter to his proposed book (after a lengthy description of events from his capture to arrival at Döberitz) Surrey Dane is soon on to his hobby-horse of 'outwitting the Hun'.

Within a very few days of our arrival, the Jerries decided to exploit prisoners of war by forming them into labouring gangs. The butcher who, a bare two months ago, had been hacking and vending his joints, the chauffeur, the lawyer, the inkslinger, the counter-jumper, the student, now became odd-job men, navvies, roadsweepers, dustmen, scavangers, coal-heavers and the like. In those early days the Jerry did not display the cunning and ingenuity he later developed in discovering degrading and obnoxious work.

This state of things was not at all in keeping with our own ideas and dodging work – 'dodging the column' or 'swinging the lead' as it was called – became the most closely studied object in camp.

The favourite retreat of the work-dodger was the camp latrine. Not that there was any privacy about this; it was near the road and open to the gaze of passers-by, male and female alike. But it served its purpose for a while for some few of us.

Failing the latrine, the alternative method was to play animated 'Hare and Hounds' with the guards, who attempted to round us up as we dodged round the tents, slipping in and out of the torn sides which we cursed at other times for letting in the rain. Their loaded rifles and bayonets gave them a big advantage. The Germans finally stopped this method of evasion by increasing the number of hounds and reinforcing them with an under-officer, armed with a heavy horse whip.

When the camp at Döberitz became better organized, dodging the column demanded cunning and craft, as the prisoners were paraded into companies every morning against a nominal roll and marched straight to work. To evade work in the face of such precautions required ingenuity. It was, however, done.

For some time at the end of 1915 the Jerries were completely baffled by the mysterious disappearance of several prisoners and their subsequent sudden reappearance in the camp. Some of the barracks were built on a slight hill, the top end of the huts being on ground level whilst the bottom end was underpinned so as to give a level floor. This left a big space at the bottom end between the earth and the barrack floor.

Some enterprising spirits prised up the floor-boards and lowered themselves down into the vacant space and found it occupied only by the usual prison rats. Next morning before parade they supplied themselves with some sacks, candles, a pack of cards and some food, and again retired beneath the floor. As the working party returned from work they came out of hiding.

They were, of course, reported as missing on parade and the usual pantomime search was made without avail. It was assumed they had escaped and their description was broadcast to the police. After a few days, one of them voluntarily appeared on parade. He was pounced upon and an explanation demanded as to where he had been. He entirely flabbergasted the Hun by maintaining that he had been nowhere but had been on parade every day. When a second accomplice reappeared the puzzled Boche concluded he had escaped but by bribery had succeeded in regaining the camp. Both were given cells and reprimanded not to vanish again.

Some of the most persistent work-dodgers were made the victims of our introduction to the punishment of 'sticky-stand', being trussed shoulders, hands and feet to a pole in full view of the camp. Snow and rain were regarded as merely incidental. The first offenders suffered so badly that they became unconscious and were removed to hospital. Later we were to become all too familiar with some vicious improvements of 'sticky-stand' and its poor relation, 'stilly-stand'.

One Russian prisoner was publicly flogged in camp. The unfortunate was bent over a form in the centre of the camp and his wrists and ankles tied together. Three of his own compatriots were ordered to give him three lashes apiece. In the hope that in their hands the lash would be lighter, they took the job. The first was accused of being too lenient in his first effort and was forced to give a double dose.

An Englishman was also punished before the camp – but for a crime committed against fellow-Englishmen. Half-starved and ill-clad as we were, stealing amongst some became common, and food and clothes had to be watched with both eyes. By night we slept with our bread beneath our heads and by day we carried it wherever we went.

The Englishman in question was caught stealing the 'rooty' [bread] of another prisoner. He was given the option of a court-martial by us or of being reported to the Germans and chose the former. A court was formed under a naval Chief Petty Officer. The sentence was that the thief had to run the gauntlet. When the poor wretch saw the businesslike avenue of prisoners lined up with knotted and wetted towels ready to give him a rough passage, his craven heart sank and he refused to face the music. The threat of reporting him to the Germans was carried out.

Their punishment was considerably more calculated and subtle than ours. He was made to stand to a pole throughout a whole afternoon facing a loaf of bread placed before him on the ground. He had been deprived of his food for the day, and the real subtlety of the punishment lay in the fact that he was not tied to the pole and only the sinister proximity of a rifle and bayonet prevented him from seizing the loaf and devouring it.

A work-dodging ruse which Surrey Dane describes as having met with the most permanent success was that of masquerading as a non-commissioned officer.

To the uninitiated it should be explained that there are two kinds of stripes worn on the sleeve by the English soldier – those V-shaped ones carried in the middle of the upper arm denoting rank and those like a V upside-down near the cuff denoting long service without rank. According to International Convention, prisoner NCOs of the rank of corporal or upwards should not be forced to work. Several of our men who had long-service stripes took advantage of this by stripping off the long-service chevrons and sewing them on upside down and higher up the arm – thus appearing as corporals or sergeants. These were known amongst us as 'buckshee' corporals to distinguish them from the 'pukka' corporals.

Any long-service man could always dispose of his stripes for a very handsome fee, usually in terms of bread and 'fags', to someone wishing to become a 'buckshee' NCO. In this way many of our men managed to avoid work during the whole of their captivity, although the records were later tightened up to prevent further self-promotions taking place when large supplies of yards of stripes arrived from Blighty.

On one *kommando* in Russia, when I was employed making a light railway, nearly every one of the NCOs was 'buckshee'. It was against regulations to make them work but the Germans did the next best thing by making them go out with working parties and stand about doing nothing. This was in the middle of the Russian winter when the thermometer was well below zero, and cases of frostbite and fainting were daily occurrences. These NCOs had to loaf about under these conditions for the whole day, as it was naturally against their principles to work even to keep warm.

They decided one day to face the possibility of a shooting party and to go on strike. They were hauled before the camp *kommandant* who reported them to Higher Authority, which in turn ordered them to be court-martialled at the Army Head-quarters at Libau. Before appearing there, they were ordered to have a hair cut.

There was amongst them a buckshee corporal, Cullen, of the Queen's (West Surrey) Regiment, who had a big growth of hair. Instead of having it all cropped he left a small full-length circular patch right on the crown of his head. When it came to his turn at the court-martial he stepped into the witness-box with his top-notch of hair well greased and standing straight up like an attenuated spike.

The judge immediately demanded to know the cause of the extraordinary head-dress, to which Cullen replied with perfect composure that he was a Hottentot and that this particular method of dressing the hair was one of the customs of their religion. He was then asked if he had anything to say in his defence for refusing to parade with the working party. Cullen explained with the greatest gravity that the strike took place on a Thursday, which was celebrated by the Hottentots as their Sunday, and that it was therefore impossible for him, on purely religious grounds, to go to work.

Along with the other NCOs, Cullen got five years' servitude in the fortress at Cologne. But he had the last laugh. When the exchange of officers and NCOs was arranged early in 1918, a special clause was inserted to the effect that prisoners undergoing terms of imprisonment in fortresses should be released first. And Cullen was amongst the very first to be sent to Holland.

Another work-dodging eccentric mentioned by Surrey Dane was also encountered in Russia in 1916.

We were quartered in the cowsheds and piggeries of a farm which had a chimney in the yard. Pitch dark and open at the top, it had been used for smoke-curing our former inmates – the pigs. On the day of our arrival this was occupied by Sergt 'Paddy' Oliver of the East Surreys. He seldom left his corner, never appeared on parade and his presence in camp was entirely unknown to the Germans for weeks. When one day he appeared on parade, the Jerries refused to have anything to do with him, so he again retired into the oblivion of his chimney.

He had served for several years in India and one of his daily amusements was to gather three or four kindred spirits into the darkness of his chimney. A piece of string nailed to the wall and lighted would be allowed to smoulder. Before this they would have a mock religious ceremony, abasing themselves to the earth, and loudly chanting unintelligible gibberish to the great mystification of the guards, who thought Oliver was mad and left him more than ever alone.

The commonest way of dodging the column was 'going krank' – reporting sick.

Most of us had a serviceable affliction which could be relied upon to give a sporting chance of a day's excused duty. In my case I had a useful and accommodating ear.

One morning, wishing to dispose of an accumulation of 'dhobying' (washing dirty clothes) I decided to report sick with pains round the heart. I paraded with a sick party and, whilst waiting for the doctor, I decided to shed my heart trouble and to complain instead of violent pains in the right ear.

As often happened the doctor did not put in an appearance.

The German *Unteroffizier* entered our names and complaints in a book and gave everyone a yellow, green, pink or white pill, and sent them off to work. When my turn came he gutteralized violently and ordered me to stand to one side.

I had visions of several days '*strafe*' for malingering, but to my great astonishment he ordered me to the main hospital. On arrival they gave me a suit of hospital clothes, cut every particle of hair off my body, and gave me the first real bath I had had for a year and a half. I was then put to bed in the ward and an orderly syringed my ear, placed a pad of cotton wool over it and covered my head with bandages and safety pins. No one examined the ear until two days later. Even then it served me well. It was a fortnight before I was returned to camp as '*Arbeitsfahig*' (fit for duty).

Quite a large number of men were in hospital as mental cases after suffering the brutalities and privations of prison life, and at a later date when I was in hospital with dysentry I had to sit up every other night to keep watch over these mental cases, to see they did not attempt to strangle themselves, cut their throats or hurl themselves from the windows.

Apart from these cases were a sprinkling of those feigning sickness or madness in an endeavour to be sent to Switzerland or Holland on the international exchange of sick which took place now and again. One man feigned a novel form of madness by conceiving a violent liking for a brick. Wherever he went the brick accompanied him; he even went so far as to take it to bed. By day he would trail the brick behind him on a piece of string, at times pretending it was a dog and barking at it. One day as the doctor was passing he tossed the brick in the air and 'headed' it as it came down. On another occasion, when the doctor had inoculated him, he solemnly produced the brick and requested that that also should be inoculated. He persevered and I believe was finally rewarded by being exchanged.

The most amusing cases were those of a private in the Royal Scots and a bugler in the King's Own Yorkshire Light Infantry who were messmates and who decided to test out the potentialities of epileptic seizures as a means of evading work. At intervals they threw dummy fits and were given temporary camp employment in consequence. This was, however, precarious as they were liable to be reported as fit for duty, particularly as this camp doctor had an absolute disregard for the sufferings of the prisoners.

They decided therefore to stage a little effect that would suitably impress the doctor with the graver aspects of epilepsy. Accordingly on the next day, as the doctor was crossing the parade ground, the young bugler, having previously filled his mouth with Kolynos tooth paste foam, dashed out and, when a few yards from the doctor, fell upon the ground and started to kick out his legs and arms violently in all directions.

At the appointed moment four stalwarts dashed out to his assistance, but in the frenzy of his fit he lightly hurled these aside. They managed eventually to secure him, as 'chucking a dummy fit' is exhausting work. The epileptics both reported sick the next day and were given permanent light camp work.

At Libau in Russia in 1917 we were employed as stevedores working on the docks: humping sacks of salt, sugar or corn was heavy going from early morning till late at night, and the usual attempts were made to 'dodge the column'.

We had at that time in charge of us an *Unteroffizier* Braun, commonly known as 'Knock-out Brown' on account of his summary habit of manhandling prisoners. Medical attention was scarce and often no doctor visited us for days. On these occasions Knock-out himself would take the sick parade and, although his methods were generally crude, he had one or two clever dodges.

One of these was in weeding out malingerers with 'a shooting pain in the back', which for a short while was a well-favoured complaint as the doctor had been sympathetic to such cases.

Knock-out made these men strip to the waist and then, passing his hands over their backs, made them indicate the exact spot where the pain was located. This spot he marked with a smudge from one of his fingers which he had just rubbed on the sole of his boots. The men were then stood on one side until the rest of the sick had been dealt with.

Knock-out then went over their backs again and made them indicate afresh the exact spot of the pain. This usually caught the malingerers napping, as they had not reckoned on a second test and had completely forgotten the exact spot previously indicated. On the second count they usually located their hurt several inches away from the first spot, and were quickly hustled off to work.

One obstructive ploy described by Surrey Dane as being widely practised by British PoWs is also referred to by Farrant.

On each occasion when we went to a fresh camp particulars of each man were recorded, name, regiment, next of kin, occupation etc. In order to give the Germans as little assistance industrially as was possible, the men, instead of giving their correct trades, used invariably to give some fancy occupation: such as hangman, robber, poacher, milestone inspector, beer tester, lion tamer, submarine ticket puncher, jigsaw puzzle maker, hair-oil mixer, pill-coater, breeder of cheese mites, inventor of chess gambits etc.

One, putting down his occupation as that of painter, was requested to furnish further particulars of his trade, and whether he was a decorator or artist. He drew himself impressively to his full height. 'Tell them,' he said with dignity, 'that my precise vocation in life is the painting of eyes on rocking horses.'

Surrey Dane records that the question he was invariably asked, on his return to England, about his PoW experiences was, 'What did you *do*?' He proceeds to itemize the occupations he was actually engaged in during his four years' servitude:

To make a start: teacher, interpreter, clerk. Then came: dustman, road sweeper, sewerage worker. Most predominant job of all was as navvy: navvy on a railway, navvy on road making, navvy on bridgemaking, on drainage, in a chemical factory, in a brick factory. Some of the other jobs would be classified as follows: farmer's boy, stable lad, bricklayer's mate, blacksmith's striker, baker's boy, coal heaver, brick and tile maker, stone-breaker, carpenter, woodchopper, gardener, fruit picker, scavenger. The queerest job I ever did was near the coast of the Gulf of Riga, haymaking knee-deep in water and under fire from Allied aeroplanes every fine day.

Of all the occupations listed by Surrey Dane, that of interpreter stands out as qualifying for an award in the art of dodging the column. It came about at Döberitz, a few months after his capture.

Early in 1915 they called for volunteers who could speak German to act as interpreters to working *kommandos*, on the understanding that such interpreters should not have to work. I had taken German at school but my knowledge of the language for practical purposes was nil. As a prisoner I had made a point of avoiding any attempt to revive the forgotten words and declensions, partly because we held everything German in contempt, partly because of a cheery optimism which insisted that peace and Blighty were just round the corner of the few weeks ahead.

Somehow or other, however, my name got on the list, and one day towards the end of April, I was warned to stand by for a speaking test in German. As this meant a 'stand easy' for the rest of the day I was nothing loth. For this privilege any one of us would have cheerfully attempted a conversation in the whole gamut of languages ancient or modern.

During the morning I strolled over to the office and found one of the German interpreters seated at his desk. As I entered he glanced up and staccatoed, '*Ja, was woolen Sie?*' This was too much of a backhander and I decided it was more discreet to attempt preliminary negotiations in my mother tongue.

'I was told to report here regarding interpreters for working parties,' I said.

'You must some other time come,' he replied. 'I am today too busy.'

I made my escape whilst the going was good, and optimistically reported to the Sergeant-Major that I had been instructed on no account to go out to work until further orders, as they might require my valuable services as an interpreter at any moment.

By evading the searching eyes of those in authority, I enjoyed a fortnight of comparative ease. Then I was awakened early one morning, about 4.30 am, and warned to be ready to leave in an hour's time as interpreter to a working party. This was considerably more than I had bargained for, and I tried to make application to be released from the job on the grounds that I could not speak the language. The fact that I was listed as an interpreter, however, was taken as sufficient evidence of my ability to 'speak the bat'.

A hectic hour was spent in packing my few belongings and exercising the few German words I knew. As I left the camp, I shouted to one of my friends a request that became something of a classic: 'For God's sake send me a German dictionary!'

We were a party of sixty, mostly Royal Marines and Sappers. After a train journey and a long march we reached our destination dog tired, hungry and dispirited. Having a particularly heavy pack, I was one of the last and arrived worn out and blown of wind to find the interpreter in noisy demand.

I doubled to the front to find our future task-master, August Durre – one of the most repulsive looking men imaginable. About five feet, nine inches high, he appeared a corrugated succession of chins which recurred later down his body as a stomach. The stomach earned for him an immediate christening from the troops of 'Guts'. The face was hard, determined and bullying. Eyes which never seemed to blink and a thin mouth fringed by a moustache, close cropped except at the ends, where it drooped walrus-like to either side.

Without further formality he asked if I spoke German, to which I returned the usual lie. He yapped out a lot of instructions in a loud, staccato monotone, none of which I understood. However, I felt I ought to perform and turned to the boys and made a few generalities, which appeared to satisfy him. As a final instruction, he asked if among us there was a '*Tischler*', as he could employ one.

'*Tischler*' conveyed nothing to me, and I asked Guts what it meant but his explanation skittled my vocabulary and was unintelligible. We seemed to be at a deadlock, and my reputation as an interpreter was fast disappearing when I had an inspiration and asked him if the '*tischler*' was for the kitchen, '*Fur die Kuche*', this last word, having relation to food, being one of the few I knew. This suggestion caused him to become so voluble that, without understanding a single additional word, I concluded I had struck the right solution. Turning to the troops, I informed them that Guts wanted a cook and asked for volunteers.

To be a cook meant never to be hungry and this ranked, with Blighty, the most lofty hope of all prisoners. The astonishment of Guts can well be imagined, therefore, when every man Jack of our party volunteered for duty as '*tischler*'. Recovering from his surprise, he chose from the bunch one, Harding, an old soldier of the Marines.

I met him next day, sagging at the knees, almost bowed double with the weight of a tree trunk on his shoulders, looking for all the world like a human 'S'. He gave me a withering look. 'Call yourself an interpreter,' he said. 'It's not a ruddy cook he wanted, but a perishing carpenter's labourer!'

Our working party was put to work in a brickyard making bricks, ten and a half hours a day for six days in the week. For me the first fortnight was spent in a kind of mental stupor, endeavouring to translate instructions and complaints in a language of which I had a profound ignorance. This state of affairs was not at all to Guts's liking and, at the end of the second week, he angrily demanded that I should abandon taking his twenty-five pfennings a day for such scanty services as were rendered under a false guise and turn to honest work with a pick and shovel.

A wordy argument ensued, Guts in German, I in English. Although he understood not a word of what I said, he had no doubt as to my meaning. The result was a complaint to head-quarters that the so-called interpreter was unable to function and asking for permission to return him forthwith.

In due course one of the camp instructors arrived from Döberitz with instructions to investigate the man. He said to me, 'They complained here that although you were sent here as an interpreter you are unable to speak German.' It seemed useless to strain his credulity by attributing my failure to temporary loss of memory, so I confessed my weakness. His scepticism was distinctly flattering.

'Surely,' he said, 'you can speak some German. I don't want to take you back. *Sprechen sie Deutsch?*'

'*Nur ein bischen,*' I ventured.

'Good enough,' he said. 'You stop.'

When the tidings were broken to Guts, he shipped himself into a voluble frenzy of indignation. Arbitration seemed the best palliative and it was finally agreed that, apart from officiating to the best of my humble capacity as interpreter, I should also perform various duties less onerous or strenuous than would otherwise have fallen to my lot.

Guts watched the departure of the camp official with beady venomous eyes which were almost waterlogged but which, withal, had the look of one who flatters himself that he is, after all, winning the consolation prize. And well they might, for he waited until but the next morning for his revenge. After the working parties had been detailed, Guts took me to one side, introduced me to a bucket and scrubbing brush and intimated, in a tone that left no room for argument, that I was henceforth to become lavatory-attendant-in-chief to the camp.

Twice during the week the lavatories had to be scrubbed, the earth-boxes emptied and the highly odiferous refuse buried. To this was added other such variegated jobs as the versatile mind of Guts could contrive. Occasionally he found a wagon or two of coal for me to unload, so that the eyes, nostrils and ears became caked. For four solid days he confined me from early morning until six at night threshing corn with a hand flail of biblical type. A solid week I spent cleaning, scouring and slicing beet, placing it in a hand press and squeezing it until the dark fluid flowed away, to be boiled into a kind of treacle for Guts's frugal Frau.

Occasionally I could get my own back. One day a much-bebraided army officer came to visit us and, whilst he was on his round of inspection, the interpreter was seen to polish and furbish his car. A well-placed nail in the off-back tyre still held the air and escaped detection. The proud double-eagle brass bonnet mascot disappeared and, although search was made for it high and low, could not be found. It now forms a very effective mount to an ash tray.

My most testing time as an interpreter came one day after we had been there some weeks when I was called out to meet a tall, dark, slim man dressed in the sombre clothes of a cleric. After the somewhat bewildering formalities of introducing ourselves and bowing several times, he talked very earnestly and at some length upon some topic unintelligible to me. I felt, however, that politeness demanded that something should be done, and I joined in here and there with a discreet *Ja, ja,* a non-committal *gewiss,* or a modest *naturlich.* After a time, the one-sided conversation flagged, the padre departed and the task of reporting the purpose of his visit had to be faced.

The few words I could identify with any degree of certainty were 'five o'clock Sunday'. It seemed safe to prophesy that the padre would look us up one Sunday—possibly next Sunday—if he had time. Punctually at five o'clock the following Sunday our friend did, indeed, appear, and I dashed out to meet him with the air of the amateur conjurer producing his first white rabbit from the top hat.

The padre asked first to be introduced to the *Herren Sergeant* and, after Alf Grange and Bill Curzons had shaken hands, we wandered into the mess room. A rowdy game of 'house' was in progress. This was hastily smothered and the men gathered round the tables whilst the padre retired to an end room, opened a bag and proceeded to don his vestments. Long before this was completed I felt in a state of pulp, realizing that he was about to hold a service with myself functioning as principal acolyte-cum-interpreter.

The opening prayer and *Onward Christian Soldiers* provided me with a breather, but the sermon which came after was a nightmare. The text and each sentence of the sermon were followed by a pause to give the interpreter the opportunity of translating. The only escape was to extemporize my own sermon and to pass this on piecemeal during the pauses left by the preacher for translation. A verse of St Matthew, written a hundred times one Saturday afternoon at school, came to my aid and provided the text and the theme.

The eloquences of the German pastor fell on deaf and uncomprehending ears; I was busy with my own exhortations. Being totally unversed in the embellishments of the pulpit, a few blunt sentences exhausted my simple theme. A collapse seemed inevitable, but 'Well, he's like the parsons at home and he's said the same again, only used different words just to drive home his point,' and 'Now he's gone over the last part once again to emphasize it', tided over the situation. Breathing more freely, we drifted into the safety of a hymn in English. Since that affair I have often wondered whether the padre, in common with the majority of educated Germans, understood English, and if so what he thought.

It was at this working party camp that Surrey Dane made tentative plans for that ultimate test of the column-dodger—escape. Along with the parcels and correspondence from home that was being forwarded from Döberitz, came letters from camp friends. The big news was the successful escape of 'Lofty' Miller of the Royal Naval Division (as mentioned by Farrant). Surrey Dane records that Miller managed to send details of his escape route to Döberitz and had also tauntingly sent coloured picture-postcards from Sweden to the Camp Commandant.

Miller's pioneering escape was a great achievement and inspired several others to try their luck. Amongst the first of these was my old messmate, Bill Parker, who chose two Frenchmen as his accomplices and who threw up a safe and comfortable job as clerk in the German office in order to make the attempt. In one of his letters to me he described very briefly what had happened and how he had reached Sioimeminde,* only to be recaptured in the docks.

This set me thinking hard, but not having the remotest idea of

* *Sic*—presumably Swinoujocie (Swinemünde).

the location of Sioimeminde, the first essential was to obtain a map. Big Bertha, one of the village women who worked in the camp kitchen, was finally persuaded to purchase a small school atlas, but the scale was so small that Sioimeminde was not shown. One of the German engineer's children, however, after a refresher of a couple of biscuits, seemed to think it was in the neighbourhood of Stettin.

The letter from Parker had been passed round, and Alf Grange, noting my covert and assiduous use of the atlas, challenged me regarding my intentions to escape and volunteered to join me—an offer I was glad to accept as he was resourceful and as sound as a rock. We decided for the present that nothing could be done but to mature our plans and complete our equipment, collecting food and making all preparations.

Our civilian disguise consisted so far of only an English cap and an overcoat, and as yet we knew nothing whatever of conditions in the world which was beyond our four walls. Grange sportingly offered to break out of camp and investigate the immediate road for getting away. The time available for doing this was short, as it had necessarily to be done at nightfall and the return made before ten o'clock, when the *appell* was carried out and the doors locked.

Clad in the overcoat over his uniform, and the English cap on his head, he slipped out at nine o'clock, went south along the main road for about two miles and across the first bridge which spanned the Oder and which we had believed to exist. Striding along in the Bond Street overcoat, with his English sporting cap jauntily set at a debonair angle, he presented a spectacle that would have excited the astonishment of even the most incurious of the local yokels.

Small wonder that on his return he was overhauled by a German soldier, apparently on leave, who attempted overtures at conversation. But Alf rejected the advances, tapped his ears and mouth as an indication that he was deaf and dumb, dropped his jaw like a half-wit, struggled with inarticulate mouthing gurgitations, waved a limp hand over the countryside, and, before his victim had recovered his balance, cut across the road into the nearest field. The ruse worked as it deserved, and just before ten o'clock Alf arrived back, breathless and covered in mud, but with the news that the road was apparently unpatrolled and the bridge unguarded.

This information was added to the stock of knowledge we were gradually accumulating for an escape. A sharp look-out was also kept for opportunities of accumulating civilian clothes. It was unfortunate for the engineer that he should have left his hat lying around. At Christmas the obliging Frieda, another of the kitchen women, lent me a skirt and shawl on the strength of some imaginative story, and the incredibly lavish build of her ample body ensured sufficient material in the skirt to provide many useful yards of civilian clothes. We had to regretfully inform Frieda that her skirt had been entirely destroyed in an unfortunate accident, but she seemed satisfied with the five marks compensation. But, as it was now the depths of a bitter winter, we decided that nothing could be done until the following May, owing to the necessity of sleeping out in the open during the nights along the escape route.

Frieda's outsize skirt material was never put to the test as civilian disguise. Shortly afterwards, in January, 1916, the working party was returned to Döberitz. In May, Surrey Dane, along with Farrant, was among the 1,000 men transferred to Russia. And one can imagine with what feelings of frustration and envy he must have heard of the bold adventures of Farrant and his three accomplices, making their bid for freedom just before all hope of escape was extinguished.

The discovery of Surrey Dane's manuscript was a moving occasion for his brother William, eldest of four Surrey Dane brothers, who himself served in the trenches during the war with the Seaforth Highlanders.

'I remember how thin and emaciated Eric looked when I met him at St. Pancras Station on his return after the Armistice,' he says. 'I am sure that his unforgettable ordeal had a profound influence on the development of his character and personality.

'Having endured so much, he had a ready sympathy and compassion for anyone in need or distress. He was also determined to repair the ravages of "the years that the locusts hath eaten". After the war he lost no time in securing his degree as a Bachelor of Commerce at Birmingham University, and all his life he was eager to acquire knowledge.

'Life dealt with him very cruelly in many ways. He lost his beloved wife, Barbara, in 1957. He became a victim of rheumatoid arthritis, had numerous operations and lived in unremitting pain. Yet he was always cheerful. His experiences as a PoW taught him never, never to complain.

'One outcome of those four wasted years of active service was the very keen part he played in voluntary military activities, to which he devoted a good deal of his leisure time. After the First World War he joined the Territorials as a gunner and held commissioned rank. In the Second World War he raised and commanded the 110th Manchester Field Regiment, Royal Artillery (T.A.). *The London Gazette* of 2 February, 1943, recorded that he had been appointed Honorary Colonel—a rare tribute.

'On the lighter side, his years of near starvation left their mark. He became somewhat of a *bon viveur* and an excellent cook. For a time he was chairman of a local branch of the International Wine and Food Society. His favourite recreation was fishing.'

In an active and successful business career, Surrey Dane rose to be Commercial Director of Peter Stubs, the hand-tool manufacturers in Warrington, Cheshire, where he spent the last thirty-two years of his life. Milestones in his career were two theses he wrote, one *The Economic History of the Staffordshire Pottery Industry*, for which he was awarded an MA by Sheffield University, the other *Peter Stubs and the Lancashire Hand Tool Industry*, later published as a book, for which he was awarded an MA by Manchester University. At the time of his death, in 1975, he was at work on a third thesis, on the Pin Industry, for the University of Liverpool. Gathering dust in the attic, the manuscript of *A Prisoner of War*, abandoned in his youth, had been long forgotten.

'Eric rarely talked about his experiences as a PoW,' recalls William Surrey Dane. 'When he did, it was invariably reminiscences about the funny things that had happened. Without doubt it was his sense of humour that saw him through with spirit unbroken, coupled with a determination to lose no opportunity to get the better of his captors. Even on the first postcard received from him at home—in which it was obligatory to say how well he was being treated—he put a flourish in shorthand under his signature which read, "We are starving".'

Chapter Three

ESCAPE FROM A COAL MINE

RIFLEMAN ERNEST EVANSON

ONE OF THE coolest and most bizarre escapes of the First World War is described in a hitherto unpublished account by Rifleman Ernest Evanson of the London Rifle Brigade, known to his comrades as 'Tich' (he was 5′ 4″). It was aboard a tram, wearing improvised civilian clothes, that he travelled the first 10-mile leg of his carefully planned escape route to Holland, after calmly walking out of a coal-mining camp in the Ruhr with a shift of German miners.

Escape has come to be regarded as a major preoccupation of the inmates of PoW camps. The first-hand accounts of escapees, mostly officers, that form the bulk of PoW literature have fostered the impression that prison-camp life revolved around the hatching of escape plots, the scooping of tunnels, the forging of documents and improvisation of equipment. It is a false impression.

Most PoWs were resigned to the fact that it was only the Armistice that would bring release. In the First World War, even though escape was a good deal easier from newly formed or improvised camps than from the purpose-built Stalags of the Second World War, it was only a very small proportion to whom barbed wire presented a challenge that called for action. Evanson records 120 individual attempts at escape within 12 months in a camp housing 2,000 as something quite remarkable.

Also to be discounted is the idea that escapees were automatically regarded as heroes by their less adventurous companions. Particularly in camps where conditions were tolerable, the punishments usually meted out on all inmates following an escape bid could make the escapee widely unpopular. Evanson describes how early escape bids from his camp led to the Germans stopping the issue of food parcels from home for a month, during which prisoners laboured down the mines on a ration of only half a pound of black bread a day.

A third illusion is that escapees were largely motivated by patriotism —a zealous desire to get back into the fight. Undoubtedly this was so in some cases, and there was the added incentive that enemy troops were being diverted from more active service to round up escapees. But from all accounts it is evident that the urge to escape was more likely to be psychologically than patriotically motivated.

'Some people have to climb a mountain "because it is there"—put others behind barbed wire and they just have to get out,' is a comparison suggested by Mr V. C. Coombs, honorary secretary of the Officer Prisoners of War (1914–18) Dining Club, many of whose members have been escapees. An RFC pilot shot down in 1917, Coombs was in the notorious Holzminden Camp during the First World War's most famous break-out, when twenty-nine officers tunnelled their way under the wire. 'Personally I took my hat off to them, despite the severe reprisals that followed,' he says. 'I was just not the escaping sort.'

Evanson's 18,000-word account of his twenty months as a prisoner of war, written shortly after his return to England when the memories were fresh, gives little indication of what impelled him to escape, even after a brutal beating-up by guards after a first unsuccessful attempt. He died in 1972, and it is his widow, Mrs Grace Evanson, who hints at the motivation.

'My husband would have struck most people as not at all the type to have undertaken such a hazardous exploit,' she says. 'He was a happy and easy-going person, who always saw the "silver lining", and considered that to complain was self-pity, which he abhorred. He was a quiet man but with a great sense of humour, amenable and uncritical of others, not at all practical in a "handyman" way, though a good planner. But if there was one thing he could not stand it was regimentation.'

Born at Crewe, Cheshire, in 1892, Evanson was employed by a City firm of accountants and had joined the Territorial Army as a raw recruit in the London Rifle Brigade in January, 1915. He sailed for France seven months later. That he had become inured to the hazards and horrors of trench warfare is evident from his laconic description of the events that led up to his capture on 1 July, 1916, the first day of the great Somme offensive. This was a day of unparalleled slaughter, when thirteen British divisions went over the top together, 20,000 were killed and 40,000 wounded, and Evanson must have accounted himself fortunate in having come through it unscathed, even if a prisoner.

The attack was launched at 7.30 am, and it was a beautifully fine day. The whole of the 56th (London Territorial) Division with the 46th Division on our left, went 'over the top' behind clouds of smoke. I was in the fourth wave and we reached our objective, this being the German 3rd line. For some reasons unknown to me, the 46th Division were not so successful, and furthermore the troops on our right also met with very great resistance. The consequence was that, quite early in the day, we were surrounded.

During the day we were attacked several times by bombing parties from each side, but these we successfully drove off. We were also troubled with snipers from fore and rear. We managed, however, to hold out until dark, this being about 10 pm. We were then very much depleted (in our sector there being some 30 or 40 men only), and so we decided to make an attempt to reach our lines under cover of darkness.

It was considered that it would be much better to go in parties of ones and twos, rather than to make a dash *en masse*. I was one of the first to start for our lines; I was quite alone. I set out knowing our men were watching my departure and waiting the opportunity to get out, but I was almost immediately challenged. I had apparently walked into a patrol lying between the German 3rd and 2nd lines. Upon making the challenge five or six Germans jumped up, and our boys, seeing the commotion in the twilight, opened rapid fire. This caused some panic among the Boche, one or two of them being hit, but luckily I escaped injury.

In their panic they threw some bombs at the trench and immediately fled, with instructions to me to follow, instead of which, finding myself alone except for the wounded Germans, I got away in another direction and so through the German 2nd line. It was some few minutes after this that I came in sight of another trench. I took this to be the front line. I waited a moment to make quite sure there was no one in the trench and then dropped in, intending to climb out on the other side, but immediately I discovered that I was not in the first line at all, but in a communication trench.

I could see the end of this communication trench and what I supposed to be the first line. I cautiously stepped to the corner in order to ascertain whether that portion of the trench was occupied and a German suddenly gripped me from the rear and I was again captured. I found he was one of a party of about sixteen men of the 55th Prussian Regiment just going out on patrol. I was then escorted through the trenches to a dressing station. I passed many piles of dead, both English and German, and it was evident that the fighting here had been very severe.

A disconcerting incident occurred when we met a German officer. He discovered that my guards had not relieved me of my bayonet and, savagely withdrawing it from my scabbard and at the same time holding me by the shoulder, threatened to stick it through me. I stood straight up and closed my eyes, feeling very 'fed up' and not caring very much at the time whether he did or not. However, he threw it away. He complained to me very bitterly in broken English that our artillery had not left one yard of their trenches intact.

At this place my hands were tied behind a cart containing two of our wounded men and we were taken across a field. During our progress the British artillery opened up on the German batteries and the driver of our conveyance started the horses off at a furious pace. It was not very comfortable for me owing to the numerous shell holes, but when they were going too fast I just lifted my feet from the ground and hung on. I was very sorry though for the two poor chaps in the cart. They were frightfully tossed about and were moaning the whole way.

I was hitched off at a large château and taken down several flights of stairs where I was interviewed by an Officer whom they addressed as General. He spoke English perfectly and at first was quite genial to me. My first thoughts when he spoke to me were 'How very English he looks'.

'What is your Regiment?' he said, and, noticing my shoulder titles, he said, 'L.R.B.—I suppose that is the London Rifle Brigade?'

I replied it was.

'And what is your profession in civilian life?' he continued. 'I suppose you are a city man?'

He seemed to know all about it so I merely nodded.

'Who do you work for in the city?' he asked, and I replied, 'A firm of accountants.' He then mentioned the name of a well-known accountant in London and his work in connection with one of the German banks and said this gentleman was a friend of his. He told me he had lived many years in London.

He then went on to ask me questions of a military nature and I was shown detailed maps of both our and the German trenches. In this way he endeavoured to get information out of me, but I stood quite still and refused to open my mouth at all. He seemed to be getting rather annoyed, and I was much relieved when he ordered me to be taken out, with the words, 'There will be more along later who will tell us more.'

Evanson's initiation into prison camp life, in a party of some 500 Somme prisoners, was at Dulmen Camp, Westphalia, where inmates worked a 12-hour day felling trees on a meagre ration of black bread and watery soup. 'It was a pretty stiff time here,' he comments phlegmatically, recording how potato peelings came to be regarded as a luxury and how he was glad of the occasional chance of dipping his hands into the swine tubs.

After six weeks he was transferred to Minden Lager, Westphalia, where the next six months proved 'the happiest days of my captivity'. Parcels from home came regularly. There was a British Army chaplain, a library, a school where men of the London Regiment taught French, German, maths and music, a band and a male voice choir of 50 voices (their favourite rendering, *Excelsior*). Through the Camp Commandant ('the best German I have ever met') he obtained a cushy job as clerk in the camp office and spent much of his time learning German.

In February, 1917, a general order was issued by the German Government saying that all prisoners of war who were fit must be put to useful work. Specifically mentioned as suitable for British PoWs were stone quarries, coal mines and salt mines. But it was under the impression that they were bound for an agricultural district to work on farms that a party of 250 British prisoners entrained in a snowstorm at dawn on 6 March. Later in the day someone remarked that they appeared to be entering a coal-mining area, and a 'chorus of groans' greeted the first mine shaft. Their destination was Westerholt Camp in the Ruhr.

When the train stopped we were drawn up outside a fairly large prison camp adjoining a coal mine. I shall never forget my first day there. As we detrained we were arranged into fours, marched into the camp and lined up in the square. There were a good many sentries present and also the Camp Commandant, together with the corporal who was second in command.

The Commandant was wearing his sword and looked very ferocious. There were several other Englishmen, who had been some time in the camp, congregated in the yard to see us in. This seemed to annoy the Commandant somewhat and he made a wild rush at the men, kicking and hitting right and left. We new arrivals naturally resented this and shouted out a protest, and the German corporal immediately spun round and made a wild rush at us, knocking one man over his kit which was placed on the ground. This seemed a bad start.

After being issued with large numbers which we were ordered to sew on our coats (they made us look like so many prize cattle) we were allowed to go into the barracks. The camp was in a very disgraceful and filthy state. There were about 2,000 men here including ourselves, among them being Russians, French and Serbians. The beds in our barrack were arranged from end to end, one above the other, in eight rows with hardly room for two men to pass in the passages between the rows. The beds consisted of coconut matting stretched between wooden uprights. With our meagre issue of blankets they were very cold indeed in the winter time. The camp square was so small that if every prisoner were in the square at the same time it would look something like a crowd at a football match.

Whilst in our barracks on this first day, we consulted together as to whether we should work or not. Some of the men being old prisoners had been in camps when the American Ambassador had visited them, and they had learned that the only work to which we might take exception was ammunition work and that coal mining was one class of work which we were obliged to do. However, after consultation, we decided not to work, hoping by refusing to be sent to another camp.

We were called out in the evening to be issued with pit clothes. When ordered to take his clothes, the first man on the list flatly refused, whereupon the Commandant ordered the sentries to set upon him. This they did with pieces of rubber about 18 inches long, the thickness of solid bicycle tyres. The man, Brookes of the Scots Guards, who had been captured in August, 1914, was promptly knocked to the ground with the rubbers. He was also kicked by the Commandant. This almost caused a riot but the cordon of sentries round the parade closed in and threatened the whole party with their bayonets.

When another man told the Commandant that he wished to see the General, the Commandant struck him saying, 'I am the General here', and had him thrown into prison. It became evident now that it was no use refusing to take our clothes. The issue proceeded and we were told off to take our different shifts down the mine next day, starting at 5 am.

Most of the work done by the prisoners was shovelling the coal onto the conveyor as the German civilian miners picked it. 'I cannot describe to you my feelings upon finding myself down below,' writes Evanson. 'The air seemed foul and oppressive and reminded me of the worst of the London tubes but several times worse. In some of the seams it was very hot indeed and it took us a long time to get used to the darkness. I shall never forget when I came up into daylight at 2 pm after my first shift, how green the trees looked, greener than I had ever noticed before. Also when going down on the afternoon shift on a bright summer's day, how bright the sunshine seemed to be.'

The first man to escape home to England from Westerholt was Private Macdonald of the Gordon Highlanders. He merely ran out of the ranks as his party was marching to the mine at 6 am one morning to make his getaway. 'Although there was a large number of guards with us, they were too astonished to fire,' Evanson records. As more and more men attempted escape (some as many as four or five times) the Germans decided to keep them apart from the other British prisoners.

They were treated much worse than the other prisoners and were known to the Germans as the 'Bad men's party'. For those who wanted to escape it was about the best possible thing that could have been done. When new men joined the party, as I was soon to do, we all got together and shared their experiences. We got to know some very valuable hints in this way. We also instituted a kind of Secret Service, and any information which could be of any use to the others, and which came to the knowledge of any one member, was duly reported to the rest. In this way we knew practically every sentry, the different hiding places in the mine, places with good cover in the neighbourhood and bridges and railways which were not guarded. Maps were freely lent and copies made wherever possible. The whole topic of conversation in the 'Bad men's party' was the best route to the border.

Evanson's first escape bid, on 16 October, 1917, in the company of Rifleman H. C. Sidwell of the London Rifle Brigade, was foiled by fog. On the fifth day of their cross-country trek they mistook a dark object looming in the fog ahead for a wood they had been looking for. It was a farmhouse. The farmer had spotted them from a window and recognized their prison clothes. He appeared at the door with a gun and a dog—and the knowledge (shared by all German civilians) that there was a reward for the capture of escaped prisoners.

We were taken back to the coal mine. I do not wish to dwell unduly upon the punishment we received, but it was very severe. Until we were tried, we were kept in prison. Here the Commandant set the bloodhounds on us. It was quite dark and we could only kick at the brutes. They made a nasty mess of our legs. Next day the sentry from whom we had escaped visited us with some of his friends and they gave us a thrashing. A day or two afterwards we were led out to be tried by an Officer who was visiting the camp. He would not listen to any complaints from us. We were sentenced to seven days' imprisonment, it being our first attempt.

For his second escape bid, on 23 February, 1918, in the company of an Australian, Private Edward Gardiner, Evanson had made much more elaborate preparations. As prison clothes had led to his capture last time, he decided that something resembling a civilian suit was an essential. After smuggling a new prison suit (blue with a thin yellow stripe) from the camp office, he used items from his food parcels to bribe the Camp Tailor, a Serbian PoW, to remove the stripe, alter the cut and replace the military buttons with civilian buttons bought from an Austrian miner he had befriended. (Prisoners were paid nominal wages for their 56-hour week in the mine.)

It was to this Austrian, in whose shift he had been working for the past four months, that Evanson was largely indebted for the success of his escape.

He appeared to be a man with a grievance. He resented the fact that his family was in Austria and he was compelled to stay in Germany. On one occasion, when complaining to me about the food conditions, he told me that in the early days of the war it was not quite so bad, as then he had done a little smuggling over the Dutch border. On hearing this I was very interested, and, having taken measure of the man, I thought I could trust him.

In any case he could not do me much harm because had he told the Germans that I was thinking of escaping again it would not have been much news to them. They knew that all men in the 'Bad men's party' would escape whenever an opportunity presented, but our supervision was as close as it had ever been and they considered that there were no loopholes left. I kept the time of my departure quite dark and told no one, except another man of our party whom I wanted to help me and who I only told the night before we went.

The Austrian did me much service. I told him I was going to escape and he seemed quite pleased and wished me good luck. I promised to bring him some soap etc. if he would help me and he very willingly consented to do so. I tried to get him to bring me a map but he told me that it was very difficult as they were compelled to register their name and address upon purchasing one and to state for what purpose it was required. However, I made a copy from an automobile map belonging to a Canadian in our party and brought it down the mine.

The Austrian pointed out to me the exact spot on the border where he had done his smuggling and explained to me that it was a bog. He gave me full details as to how to get through it and I was very excited over it. In the words of the Australian who came with me, we considered we were now on a 'Sure thing'. Through the Austrian I obtained two collars and ties, (the kind of tie that can be fixed in about half a minute), also two large German hats. I also obtained about a litre of rum which was very useful on the journey. I paid for these things in German currency which I had, but I cannot now remember what they cost. My compass I bought from the English interpreter, who had two.

During my sojourn in Germany I had picked up a good working knowledge of German and on one occasion I asked the Austrian what he thought of my German. He said, 'It is very pretty, but no one would take you for a German.' I was very sorry for this, but he told me that there were a large number of Belgian peasants at large in that part of Germany who could not speak perfect German and my foreign accent might well be taken for Belgian. I determined then that should I be questioned at any time as to my nationality I should say I was Belgian.

Another thing which had to be decided before we attempted to escape was how we should cross the River Lippe, about 25 kilometres from where we were. I had crossed this river by a bridge in the nighttime on my first attempt, but since then three Englishmen had been returned to the Camp having been caught on this very bridge. These men had their wits about them when they were recaptured and made the best of a bad job. On their way to prison they got into conversation with their captors.

'I suppose you have plenty of work to do here?' one of them asked.

'Oh yes!' replied a sentry boastingly. 'We captured nine last night and ten the previous night', and so on.

'But don't you catch a lot in the daytime?' asked the Englishmen.

'Oh no!' said he. 'We are never on duty here in the daytime. You don't suppose prisoners come over here in daylight, do you?'

The Englishmen replied, 'Oh no, of course they wouldn't', but immediately on their return to Camp they said, 'We have had a bit of bad luck, boys, but it is all right, the bridge isn't guarded in the daytime and the next time we go we shall lie up near until they have gone and then hop over quickly.'

This fact caused me to decide to go over the bridge in daylight. But 25 kilometres is a long way to walk and, as I proposed travelling the first day, it was necessary that we should get out of the neighbourhood quickly in case we should meet workmen from the mine who knew us. It was this which caused me to enquire of the Austrian regarding a tramway which ran in the direction of the bridge and which I had crossed in my first attempt. I discovered that we could travel on this tramway for about ten miles. From the Austrian I learned the starting place, how to get to it quickly, the name of the place I wished to go to, the time it would take the tram to reach it, the fare and also what I must say to buy the tickets.

The only remaining thing was to get clear of the mine, which was no easy matter. We decided upon Saturday morning as the best time. The previous night I disclosed our plans to Rifleman Sidwell, with whom I had made the last attempt. I told him we intended to give the overseers the slip and stow away down the mine. He worked in the same district down the mine as the Austrian and I, and it would be an easy thing for him, when the overseer missed us, to say that we were sick and had stayed in barracks. I felt under some obligation to him and I mapped out for him our complete route. I told him to keep this to himself for his own benefit, and that if I followed the route laid down and was successful, I would let him know.

When Saturday morning arrived, we both wore two suits. We wore our prison suit over our civilian suit, in the lining of which we carried a small store of biscuits and chocolate. We also had the collars and ties wrapped up in paper in our inside pockets and the trilby hats were rolled up down the legs of our trousers. Luckily there was no search on this particular morning and we arrived at the pithead without mishap. We were rather afraid that our bulky proportions would be noticed, but nothing happened.

When the first overseer came for his gang we saw our opportunity and slipped into the cage behind them before our own overseer had arrived. Once down below without our escort we got away easily. As it is so dark down below and each man carries a lamp, everyone looks the same from a distance and no one suspected us. We had brought lamps which belonged to men who had escaped during that week and were still away, so that should the overseer look in the Lamp Room, he would find that our lamps had not been drawn and believe the story that we were sick.

We decided to hide up in the main road. We threw two small wagons off the lines on their sides. Wagons with damaged wheels were frequently seen lying like this. We then crept into the wagons and lay there for about 24 hours, i.e. until 6 am on Sunday. When the men were changing shifts at 2 pm on the Saturday, some Germans were actually sitting on the wagons in which we were lying, but they didn't suspect anything.

At 2 pm on the Saturday, when the prisoners on the morning shift had returned to the camp, there would naturally be two Englishmen missing from the 'Bad men's party' and I had arranged for Sidwell to tell the German sentries that he had seen us going in the direction of the woods at 6 am that morning. This I have no doubt was duly carried out. The result would be that the Germans would search for us with the hounds in the neighbouring woods about sixteen hours before we actually got away, and all this time we were hiding down the mine.

During the night we took off our prison clothes and buried them. We had hidden away in a tin box underneath one of the props some civilian overalls which we had bought from a Russian prisoner, together with our map and compass. Dressed in these overalls, with large mufflers round our necks and small skull-caps on our heads, we crept out of our hiding place. We made our way to the shaft and there we saw a small queue of German miners waiting for the cage.

From 10 pm on Saturday until 6 am on Monday no prisoners worked down the mine, so that our fellow passengers in the cage on this particular morning were all civilians. We feigned sleep during the ascent, and when we reached the top we followed the crowd and handed in our lamps. Our lamps were exactly the same as the Germans' except for a small numbered tab, which we had detached whilst in the wagons. There were no sentries at all at the mine, and while the Germans went to the bath houses, we waited a favourable opportunity and got away as we were, all dirty.

We had no difficulty in getting from the mine premises as it was quite dark and no one noticed us go into the neighbouring woods. There we took off our overalls and buried them. We found a stream and, having brought some soap and a small cloth, we proceeded to wash and make ourselves fairly respectable. We put on the collars and ties, replaced the skull caps with German hats, which took rather a lot of knocking into shape before we considered them presentable, rubbed up our boots and set off to find the tram.

It was the first tram of the day, which left about five minutes after we had sat down. As it was early on Sunday morning, it was not very well patronized. The seats were arranged across the car and we sat on the first two seats inside, opposite each other, and very diligently looked out of the window the whole way, in case anyone should feel inclined to get into conversation with us. We also kept our feet under the seats because we were very afraid people might notice we were wearing good boots, there being very few in Germany.

The most exciting incident of the tram ride occurred when, going through a large town, the wheels began to slip. It was a wet day and the car was unable to take the hill. My Australian friend was sitting on a single seat near the door and the conductress came in and said to him in German, 'Excuse me, I want to get the sand.' His knowledge of German was not great, and not having any idea at all of what she wanted, he thought the best thing to do was to offer her his ticket in case she had come to inspect it. I heard what she said, and although I had no idea where the sand actually was, it occurred to me that it must be under his seat, so I said to him in the best German I could, 'Stand up'. He did this, and the lady lifted the seat and took out the sand, and the incident closed.

We reached our destination quite safely, and on alighting from the car, we had a great desire to run, but we held ourselves in check and walked steadily forward along the main road.

It was a very small village and we soon found ourselves on the highway. We came across a sign-post pointing out the direction of the town upon the river where we were to get over the bridge. We reached the bridge about 10 am on Sunday and found it unguarded.

Once over the bridge, it was necessary for us to walk boldly through the town as there was no other way. It was a fairly large military town, and when partly through it, we heard the sound of an approaching band. This turned out to be a regiment of infantry going, I should think, to Church Parade. We were walking on the road at the time and a policeman ordered us onto the footpath to get out of the way of the troops. I thought at the moment that we were discovered. We didn't answer him but got quickly out of the way. We heaved a sigh of relief when we eventually got clear of the town into the country again.

It was about half past eleven when, being in a lonely part of the country, we entered the woods for a rest and something to eat. I recognized the locality as I had been in the same wood in my first attempt, and after eating some biscuits and chocolate, we settled down to study our map and make quite sure of the road we intended to take, although we were both very tired, due probably to the great excitement and also to the lack of sleep the previous night. Sleep now, however, was entirely out of the question. We both felt that we had done very well so far and had made up our minds that this time we would spare no effort to get right through.

We arranged to travel the rest of the journey entirely by night. We also arranged that, should we be challenged *en route* by any person unarmed, we should refuse to halt and make a run for it. Should the person be armed, we considered it more prudent to allow ourselves to be captured, but the Australian suggested that on a given signal, I should trip up our captor and he would knock him out. There was no necessity for this, however, as we were never challenged although we passed several people.

We kept to the woods as much as possible, following our route absolutely as we had planned it. We had arranged to take five minutes halt each hour, but it was a great temptation when we found ourselves going well not to do this. The consequence was that we travelled from 7 pm until midnight on Sunday without any halt at all, and then it came very suddenly.

Some fortnight previously I had a nasty boil on the instep of my right foot which had been cut by the German doctor. The wound was closed but my foot was still swollen and inflamed, and I carried a small spare roll of bandage in my pocket. It must have been the pain this foot caused me, and the fatigue of the journey, which caused me to faint. I collapsed in the road soon after midnight.

When I came round, Gardiner was giving me water and I really felt that I should never be able to walk again. He tried to rouse me by saying that if I didn't pull myself together we should be recaptured. I felt it was no good, however, and I offered him the map and said that as I couldn't walk any further it was no good both of us being captured, so I advised him to get off alone. He would not listen to this, and said as we had started together we should stick together.

He dragged me off the road behind some bushes, and there he took off my boot and had a look at my foot. Although water was very scarce, he almost emptied our water bottles on my bandage and bound up my foot again with this cold water dressing. My foot now felt much better, and after having a sip of rum and a rest for about half an hour, I felt that I could start again slowly. It was much too cold to lie for very long.

He gradually quickened the pace and we went for another two days without further incident. At 6 o'clock on Tuesday morning we lay up in a wood within sight of the River 'An'. It was from this river that we were to find the path which ran straight into the bog.

We started our last trip at 7 pm on Tuesday and followed the river. We struck the bog about 9 pm. The path round this river was one of the most difficult we had, owing to the dense undergrowth in the woods on the banks. We took our direction very carefully and set off to wade through the bog.

It was not very deep when we entered, but on two occasions we thought we were going down. It was very heavy going indeed. I think we must have crossed the border shortly after midnight. We knew that, from the point of striking the bog, if we kept our proper direction, we were 2½ kilometres from the border and 5 kilometres from the end of the bog. It was about 3 kilometres wide, and I think we must have travelled absolutely through the centre.

About 3 am the ground began to rise and we were soon on dry ground. We came across a small bush and decided to take a rest. I said to Gardiner, 'We are in Holland now or I'm a Dutchman!' He was inclined rather to be cautious and wouldn't hear of our walking about openly. It was a much too serious matter now to give the Germans any more chances.

After about five minutes here we continued on our way in the same direction and presently struck a railway. It was running due north and I advised walking along it, as I firmly believed we were in Holland. He wouldn't hear of this and we kept to the ditches in following the railway. He noticed that the telegraph poles were very different from the German, but didn't consider this was sufficient proof that we were really in Holland.

After about a quarter of an hour we came across a level crossing. There was a printed notice on it and I decided to go and see what it was all about. I did so, leaving Gardiner in the ditch, and you can judge my delight when I discovered that it was in Dutch and not in German. I called him over and he came very cautiously, and then we decided we were really in Holland.

We followed the main road after this and there was a light in the first house we saw. Gardiner said to me, 'Go and knock at this door and ask if we are in Germany or Holland.' I should never have consented to do this had I felt we were in Germany, but although we believed we were in Holland, we hardly dared take it for granted.

I knocked at the door, which was answered by a workman. I asked him in German if this place was in Germany or in Holland. He said, 'Holland, Holland!' and Gardiner immediately held out his hand saying in English, 'Put it there, Old Sport, you're a Toff!' We begged a box of matches as ours had become too damp for use, and we went on our way rejoicing. We gave ourselves up to the Dutch police at Enschede.

Owing to the regulations, we were kept in the Quarantine Camp in Enschede for sixteen days before being handed over to the British Consul at Rotterdam. Our treatment here was excellent; we were provided with a good bed with white sheets (the first I had seen for 2½ years) and splendid food (four meals a day). In addition to this we received six bars of chocolate and ½ lb apples per man daily and cigarettes and cigars were provided to any extent. We felt we were in heaven.

There is not much more to say. We were taken to the British Consul in Rotterdam, who rigged us out in a new civilian outfit, and we were put up at the Hotel Harwich, where we stayed nine days. This was our first real taste of freedom after being twenty months in captivity, and we appreciated it to the full.

As with most escape stories, the sequel comes as an anticlimax. Evanson spent the rest of the war with the Army Accountancy Corps in Blackpool and Woolwich, being promoted to RQMS. After being demobilized in 1919, he married the girl he had met while at a training camp in 1915 and whose letters and food parcels had done much to keep his pecker up in the prison camps.

Family and work absorbed the rest of a successful, contented, uneventful life. For 44 years from 1919, Evanson served with United Dairies Ltd, rising to become Secretary, and (after a merger) Joint Secretary of Unigate Ltd. In a house magazine tribute, on his retirement in 1963, it is difficult to equate the scheming 'Tich' Evanson of the Bad Men's Party at Westerholt with the pin-striped instigator of 'office machines for dividend payments', the promoter of benefit societies and a staff pension scheme.

'He regarded his escape as the biggest thing he ever did, though he rarely talked about it,' says Mrs Grace Evanson. 'If his war experiences had any lasting effects it may have been that he always liked doing things in comfort. No camping out and roughing it on holidays for him! He was the best husband you could have—always generous, never critical of others, never saying "No" if it could be "Yes". I do miss him still.'

Among mementoes she treasures at the home in Horsham, Sussex, he retired to—the Military Medal he was awarded, photographs of their three sons (one killed in the RAF in the Second World War), daughter and five grandchildren, holiday snaps in South African and Mediterranean sunshine—is a tailpiece to the escape story she found among his papers. It refers to that promise he had made on the eve of his escape to Rifleman Sidwell, his partner in his first escape bid.

While in the Quarantine Camp, I began to think of the friends I had left behind me in the coal mine and how I was to let Sidwell know I had reached Holland safely by the route which I had given him. Obviously I could not use my own name in writing to him, as it would undoubtedly have been recognized by the German censors. I hit upon a notion and from the Dutch town of Enschede I sent the following postcard through the Dutch post:

'Dear Rifleman Sidwell,
I am in Holland in the interests of repatriated British Prisoners of War and I hope to see you here soon. I trust you have read my book, *The Appointed Way*, and that it will do you good as it is the only true path.

Yours sincerely,

(Rev) Ernest Tich.'

'Tich' was my Nom de Guerre, and I knew that should he receive this card it would fully explain itself. I afterwards received a letter from him addressed to the 'Rev Ernest Tich' at my home address and I then knew that he had received my message from Holland.

If Rifleman Sidwell ever did attempt to follow in Tich Evanson's steps along that true path across the frontier bog, it was only to be recaptured. Mrs Evanson recalls that it was not until after the war that he was repatriated. Her husband kept in touch with him for some time, and he would undoubtedly have heard of the later exploits of the Bad Men's Party. A respectable white-collar worker again, he would have listened as to news from another existence, increasingly remote as he became absorbed back into the 'real' world of accountancy.

Chapter Four

ANYONE FOR TENNIS?

CAPTAIN DOUGLAS LYALL GRANT, MC

BY COMPARISON WITH other-rank prisoners of war, officers led a life of almost pampered ease. Their grouses centred on such things as the quality of the wine, the availability of tennis courts, the shortcomings of the orderlies who waited on them.

But being treated as gentlemen of enforced leisure rather than as slave labourers—all play and no work—had its drawbacks. Boredom was the big problem. And life behind barbed wire for this privileged class could be just as much a test of character and mental stamina as in the working camps of the downtrodden Tommy.

'Anything is better than to allow oneself to become like some people who spend most of their days in bed and are quite beyond doing anything', writes Captain Douglas Lyall Grant, MC, in the diary he kept throughout his two years' captivity. Even an exuberant extrovert like himself found the going tough at the start. 'The only thing is to make the best of a bad job and when down in the mouth think of Jonah—he came up all right.'

The almost daily entries in Lyall Grant's diary, amounting to over 50,000 words, give the fullest, and easily the liveliest, account of the goings on in officers' camps in Germany of any that have come to light. If his reactions cannot be regarded as altogether typical, it is because he was himself a character out of the ordinary. At a crowded memorial service after his death in 1968, shortly before his 80th birthday, a fellow territorial officer in the London Scottish Regiment said of him, 'Duggie went through life with a flourish—with great panache. He was always a gay cavalier.'

Like the majority of First World War officers, Lyall Grant was a product of the public schools and there is evident satisfaction in his observation after initiation into his first PoW camp: 'It is very like being at school again'. Though 28 at the time, a married man, the boyish high spirits of a popular public school boarder give a glow to what from another pen might be a grey, even despairing, commentary.

Games (from rugger, cricket, tennis, to fives, golf, bridge), and theatricals (in which he excelled in comic roles) are his mainstay. The equivalent of feasts in the dorm are indulged in whenever feasible. Prefectorial privileges attend his election to an exclusive club in one camp known as 'The Apostles'. Cocking a snook at authority is a point of honour (like the time he was hauled before the Commandant for doing the goose step on parade and solemnly explained that, as some are born with a stammer, he was born with a 'peculiar walk').

A Londoner of Scottish parentage, educated at Trinity College, Glenalmond, in Scotland, Lyall Grant exulted in his Scottish connections, though he himself had little trace of a dialect. He learns with deep concern of heavy casualties to the London Scottish Regiment during the Somme offensive, launched a month after his capture. As an act of patriotic defiance he takes every opportunity to play his bagpipes at the head of a ceremonial parade. And it is concealed inside the bag of his pipes and sewn in the waistband of his kilt that he eventually smuggles out his secretly written diary notebooks.

Though the diary was soon forgotten (few of his family were aware of its existence), the spirit of camaraderie that pervades it remained the driving force in his life. An unexceptional career in banking and commerce was of secondary importance to his family life and the three institutions to which he gave a lifelong loyalty—his old school, his old Regiment and the London Scottish Rugby Football Club. 'No one was dull when Duggie was in the party' was a tribute paid at the memorial service that links back to the days when he helped boost morale on the playing fields and theatre boards of Gütersloh and Crefeld, Schwarmstedt and Holzminden.

As much as in the trenches, it was in these dreary backwaters of the war that the public school ethos was put to its severest test. And in reading Lyall Grant's breezy and buoyant account it should be remembered that there was another side to the picture. Apart from noting their existence, he does not refer again to those unfortunates who had apparently succumbed to despair, 'quite beyond doing anything'. There is no allusion to the introvert, the intellectual, the aesthete, who must have been as much a part of a PoW camp as of a public school. Sex scarcely rears its head, apart from jocular references to actors in drag ('the girls looked ripping').

From a book-length diary with few dull pages, it is possible here to give only representative extracts from the four camps where Lyall Grant served his captivity before being repatriated to Holland in April, 1918. Little can be gleaned about his early experiences on the Western Front, except that he landed in France in September, 1914, with the London Scottish, fought at Messines and was awarded the Military Cross, and that at some stage he was appointed Embarkation Officer at Boulogne.

The early entries are given fully, partly because the bizarre nature of Lyall Grant's capture is so engagingly in character, partly because they hint at the slough of despond from which (unlike the less resilient) he succeeded in rousing himself. The diary, which must itself have been a morale-booster, is headed: 'This Was Started In My Room At Douai The Day After My Capture'.

2 June, 1916. All the best captives write a diary, so what more fitting than that I should keep one. Whether it will be allowed or not remains to be seen.

Well, little did I think on leaving home yesterday morning that by seven I should be in German hands. For one reason and another we were unable to leave Farnborough until after lunch, when we set off in a 200 hp Rolls Royce, the pilot being one who had never been to France before and whose career there as a free man certainly proved to be a short one.

I enjoyed every moment of the flight across the Channel at 7,000 feet and in fourteen minutes. We passed over Boulogne and I could distinctly see the Quai where the gods have apparently decreed that I shall work no more. From Boulogne to St Omer the way to one who knows it should be plain, but apparently the pilot lost it and at 4.15, one hour and three-quarters after leaving, I was surprised by guns opening fire on us. The pilot dived to show that we were British as he, like I, thought they were our own anti-aircraft guns which have been known to make similar mistakes before.

So steeply did he go that I, unaccustomed to aeroplanes, thought that we were falling and that he had been hit, but on looking round saw that he was still all right. At about 500 feet the engine gave out, the shells were all round us and the machine was hit in many places. As we neared the ground I could see that he was making for a more or less clear field below. To reach this we had to avoid some telegraph poles but after crashing through the wires, when my face was saved by the gun mounted in front of me, we struck a post and turned to land upon our nose. Although the front of the machine where I was sitting was wrecked, I was thrown clear and escaped with a shaking, and got up cursing our gunners to receive the surprise of my life in finding ourselves surrounded by Boches.

Our first remarks will stick in my head for many a long day. The pilot said, 'I'm awfully sorry to have brought you to this,' and I replied, 'Don't you worry, but it's my wife and people I'm thinking about'; and then (to show how one's mind drifts even in the most serious moments) my next remark was, 'I wish that I had gone to the dentist when I was at home.'

By this time an officer who spoke English had turned up, closely followed by two others in a small car, and upon my requesting to be taken away from the crowd we were put in this and driven to what appeared to be Brigade HQ, where we had cigarettes and met another officer with whom I conversed in French. From there we drove to a large château where we had wine and sandwiches and met several English-speaking Germans, also the gunner of the battery that brought us down; he had been seven years in Sheffield so spoke English excellently.

After an hour there we were motored to Lille Station in charge of an officer, sergeant and one man, and we all got into a 2nd class carriage *en route* for Douai. Life in Lille appeared to be normal and the French showed every sign of friendliness to us, waving and blowing kisses. I wonder how long it will be before anyone throws kisses to me again! I expect bricks will be more like it.

On arrival at Douai a very short walk brought us to some barracks, where we took farewell of our guard who throughout had been most friendly, the sergeant insisting on my accepting cigars from him, and were placed in separate rooms. I had supper consisting of beer, black bread and cheese, and then rolled on a bed of straw—a slight change from the one I had risen from twelve hours before.

Today has been one of the hardest, a continual fight against depression. I never knew that a heart could be so heavy and it mustn't be carried on the sleeve. To my guards I appear the most cheery of mortals and greet them all in French, but to myself I'm in the depths of despair. Solitude was never pleasing to me, and when one has nothing to read, nothing to see, and nothing to do but think of 'this time a week ago!' and the like, it takes all one's time to keep back an ever-rising lump and I never realized before how nearly mental sickness could make one physically sick . . .

This afternoon I was interviewed by a Flying Corps officer who was at Oxford and who proved to be quite nice and promised that a note should be dropped tomorrow to say that we were O.K. I hope that it is picked up all right so that those at home may know that I am safe; I believe worrying about them is one of the worst parts of the whole business. He told me that we would soon be sent to Germany where we would have quite a good time; as Mr Asquith said, 'Wait and see!' His job was to pump me, but after I had replied, 'I don't know' to various questions, he showed excellent sense by shutting his book and remarking, 'Anyhow, if you did know you wouldn't say, but that is what I am here for.'

3 June. Another day of much internal fighting against the depression that must not be allowed to get the upper hand. It's no good crying over spilt milk, and the only thing is to make the best of a bad job and when down in the mouth think of Jonah—he came up all right . . .

The day has been a very long one, broken only by half-an-hour's exercise in the prison yard, and a visit from a Bavarian Duke or something who told me there had been a great naval battle in which we lost 116,000 tons of shipping to their 20,000. I do smile. He was rather fed up because when he came in I was lying on the bed and he said, 'Don't get up', and I didn't. We discussed the war and I remarked that as the world had been going on for so many years it was unfortunate that it should have taken place in our lifetime, but he said that he felt it a great thing to draw the sword in defence of the Fatherland. After that I had little to say to him as he was very dense and quite believed that the Huns were the attacked and not the attackers.

4 June. Another miserable day spent alone . . . I got a French novel this morning and amused myself wading through it. The food continues to be on the same lines and by purchasing a little beer and eating sugar it is just enough. Possibly this is the finger of fate pointing out to me that it is possible to live on the necessaries and not the luxuries of life. Anyhow, it ought to take off some of my superfluous flesh and that would be one advantage to place on the credit side . . .

Four days later, after a meandering two-day train trip through Belgium and Germany, Lyall Grant arrived at Gütersloh Camp in Westphalia, a quarantine centre through which most captured officers passed before being allocated to other camps. Some 750 officers were comfortably housed there, 120 of them British, the rest French, Russian and Belgian. His ten weeks there were an encouraging initiation. Though in an early entry he remarks on the days being 'appallingly alike', depression was soon submerged in the round of sporting activities, camp entertainments, mess fraternization, lessons in French and Spanish, public and private junketings, that were to be the pattern of the rest of his captivity.

10 June. We have been moved out of the quarantine building today and are now in 'B' house which is the one reserved for British officers. I have, as usual, landed on my feet and am in a room with one K— of the 9th Royal Sussex and R— of the 6th R.S.F., both excellent fellows who are doing all they can for me and have invited me to join a mess that they have with one or two others as the weekly ration here would only last an ordinary being for one day and living on it is out of the question.

I've spent most of the day looking round and in the afternoon had a game of soccer by way of a little exercise. It is very like being back at school again. Everyone, all nationalities, messes in the same building and all meals are run in two relays, but we act more or less on our own. Instead of breakfasting at 7.15 we get up at 8, attend roll-call at 8.30, and then four of us breakfast quietly in the restaurant at 9.15. We're supposed to lunch at 11.30, but stroll in at 1 and have a light lunch from the food parcels of the members of the mess, all of which are pooled. Tea is taken in the restaurant at 4.30 except on Sundays and Wednesdays when we tea in our room, and dinner at 7.30 chiefly consisting of parcel contents again. Lights are out at 10.30 but silence does not necessarily reign! We are allowed one hot bath per week.

14 June. I must say that this camp has come as a very pleasant surprise to me, being infinitely more comfortable than I had anticipated. I know half the fellows here already as the story of my capture had preceded me and it is generally agreed that it's one of the worst bits of luck of the war.

This afternoon I played my first game of hockey, and at night I was invited to pay a visit to the Russian quarters by some Russian Guards officers that I've got to know. This is usually a dangerous undertaking as their capacity for strange mixtures is enormous, but I had been warned and tasted warily. They are good fellows and those who don't speak English speak French. Most of their names appear to end in '-off'. They also appear to be all musical and all good artists. In fact there is an abundance of talent of all sorts in this camp.

16 June. The sale of all wine and beer has been stopped for a week because yesterday somebody succeeded in getting an Austrian flag and hoisted it half-mast to the great sickness of the Boche, who shows his frightfulness in this way . . .

17 June. I led off this morning with my first Spanish lesson. I'm taking them from a French officer who assures me that he speaks fluently, but from what I can make out his chief qualification as a tutor is that in pre-war days he sold ribbons and other such touching pieces of ladies' attire to the Argentine! If I do succeed in learning anything it will doubtless be with the equivalent of a Swan & Edgar accent which will fail to meet with my Spanish-speaking in-law's approval . . .

18 June. Being Sunday foreign languages were given a miss and in the morning I attended a church service held in a loft and taken by a Canadian Padre. A German was present to see that the time was not utilized in making preparations for escape, and I hope that he approved of our prayers for the King and for speedy victory over all his enemies! . . .

Each day there is a 'Budget' published, the work of the more literary and energetic of our members, chiefly consisting of translations of the various 'officials' taken from the German papers, with leading articles on any special bits of news. There is also a monthly production with short stories and illustrations which is wonderfully good. The summer number is just out, and there is a hit at me under 'Things We Want to Know': whether 'Joy Riding in an aeroplane over imperfectly known country is not an overrated amusement?'

20 June. The chief event today was the removal of the ban on wine and beer, and to celebrate the occasion, coupled with the fact that tomorrow will be the anniversary of my wedding, our room gave a 'beer'. This takes the place of giving a dinner here and one asks just a select few to discuss the affairs of nations and sing a song or two. Amongst the guests were a couple of Russians.

1 July. [Note: the first day of the Battle of the Somme.] Dominion Day, which was celebrated by the Canadians by a game of baseball in the morning and a dinner at night, both very noisy entertainments. The time between *appell* and breakfast I filled in by a visit to the dentist, a Russian noted for his heavy hands, and I for one am ready to endorse his reputation. However, he filled a tooth and I escaped alive. The French lesson got a miss for tennis and in the afternoon I watched our Hockey Team defeat the Russians 1st by 15–12, the 12 being their handicap.

3 July. Today we got the first news of the offensive which appears to be going well. Of course all that we get is through German spectacles, so to speak, and this depresses some people; personally, it cheers me because I can't help dividing all their successes and multiplying all their defeats – rather a pleasant frame of mind for a prisoner of war!

This afternoon, in company with 39 others, went for a walk. This is a new idea, mutual arrangement between British, French and German Governments, by which officers give their parole not to escape while out walking, and in return no guard is sent with them but only one man as a guide. We have parole cards which we sign and give up on our return. We go out in batches of 40 twice a week. The crops looked to be good but we saw practically no men and certainly no young ones, while the ladies of the district must be more noted for their rotundity than their beauty.

7 July. K's birthday. A team of his friends who call themselves 'The Gliders' played the French at soccer. The match was well advertised and the entire camp turned out to watch it. We marched on to the field to three chanters and two mouth organs with a banner bearing our name; we gathered in the centre of the field and gave our war cry *à la* New Zealanders. At half time an enormous jug of beer was lowered from one of the windows and the orderlies' band, in fancy costume and strengthened by much beer at K's expense, paraded round the ground. After the game, which we won 6–4, there was song, wine and beer in our room, where at times there was hardly room to move.

10 July. Cricket started today . . .

12 July. We have now been forbidden to shout at football matches, which is sad as half the fun is the barracking. The reason given is that the people of Gütersloh complained that it was not seemly while Germany was passing through such a trying time! They apparently fail to recognize that from a life and death point of view Britain is also having her share of trials, but anyhow, as the village is two miles away it must have been 'some' shouting and I expect the truth is that they think we're cheering the Allied advance on all fronts.

14 July. This being a French fête no one did any work. The Boche had told the French that they were not to celebrate it, with the result that they did so to a man, ably assisted by many of their allies. They started off with the *Marseillaise* at morning *appell* and from that minute never looked back. Most of them lunched in the restaurant and all the allied National Anthems were sung frequently and loving speeches freely exchanged. I made one in French!!

At night the band played and just on 10 o'clock a procession was formed, which, headed by a mock band with Chinese lanterns and several people dressed up as ladies, went round the camp growing in numbers until some 500 howling allies were marching round arm-in-arm. At each house a stop was made and patriotic speeches delivered from the steps. On arrival at the British House the Germans appeared with fixed bayonets in front and rear of the procession, but all but a few escaped in at the front doors and out at the back windows. It was a great scene.

19 July. Chief event today is that I discovered that I've got a broken rib. Since the last rugger game it has been very sore; the doctor looked at it today and now I'm trussed up like a mummy and find much difficulty in breathing; however, I can walk and that's a great thing, although it's rotten that I'm off games for a bit. Quite a bunch of new officers came in and a fellow in the London Rifle Brigade tells me that the London Scottish must have been almost wiped out. I hope that it isn't true but am afraid from what he says that it must be.

20 July. Received my first letter from home. Tremendous joy . . .

25 July. Visited the Art Exhibition now being held here. Everything on exhibit is made or painted in the camp and one would never believe that the hand of man could turn such extraordinary things out of nothing. A grandfather clock, made entirely out of odd pieces of wood and scraps of wire, which keeps perfect time, is only a small example of what is on view. The paintings by some of the Russian artists are magnificent. The caricatures are also good—I am on this wall. On the whole I would give the Russian section top marks with the British an easy last!

2 August. In the morning our mess had two Russians to breakfast. The meal provided by the Germans consisted of one thin slice of black bread and some washy coffee. Our menu for our guests was Fruit and Cream, Porridge, Fish, Sausages, Bacon,

Tomatoes, Various Potted Meats and Game, Toast, Butter, Jam & Marmalade – all from parcels of course.

7 August. Tennis today with two Russians, one of whom owns a little place in Russia, about half the size of France, and wants me to go there after the war for some bear hunting. He also says that he is coming to England to see me – I'll be able to show him round the back garden!

11 August. No startling events today except the arrival of my pipes . . .

17 August. Ten of us and forty French and Russians were warned at evening *appell* to move tomorrow. Much borrowing of boxes and hasty packing followed, and after dinner the camp gave itself up to much noise and I headed a large procession with the pipes. Twice round the ground and then into House 'B'. The Commandant, followed by many satellites and shrieking with rage, bore down on the crowd, but as he entered by the front door the pipes were shot out of a back window and thence to safety. Having shouted himself hoarse the Commandant vented his wrath by arresting the only man who was not making any noise and bearing him off to 'jug'.

Crefeld Camp was a former cavalry barracks on the outskirts of Crefeld, a busy town north of Dusseldorf and only some thirty miles from the Dutch border. Security was rigorous, with weekly searches for signs of tunnelling, and during his nine months there Lyall Grant records only twelve escape bids, five of them successful. He does not himself appear to have considered the possibility of escape. He was anyway soon in the swim of camp life, with scarcely a day unworthy of note.

After what he describes as 'doing the "new boy" act, wandering round and gaping', he compares the two camps (in a way that would have had any inmate of an other rank camp blinking in disbelief):

On the whole I put my money on Gütersloh, principally

because of the games. Here one can only get tennis and fives, but the latter club is full, with a big waiting list. There are some fifteen tennis courts so one can play more than at the other camp. There is a loft which is used as a gym and where single-sticks and fencing can be pursued, and now a boxing class has been started which I intend joining.

The food here is very much better and there is one large dining hall and two smaller ones, also better, but there is nothing that really takes the place of the Gütersloh restaurant. There is a bar and a small room with a coffee bar where one is waited upon by two buxom damsels. The dry canteen is far and away better and things not on sale there can be ordered from the town.

There is no common room here, which means that one does not meet so many fellows and also leads to the formation of many cliques. There is nothing to choose between the two libraries. Last but not least the Germans here are far and away nicer than those that we have just left, all obliging and polite, and everyone agrees that the Commandant is one of the best. Summing up, one might say that if one is keen on exercise and games, go to Gütersloh; if not, then come here. Personally give me London.

26 August. Went out for my first walk today. Much better than the Gütersloh efforts. We started with a 20-minute tram ride and then walked for 8 kilometres or so. The tram had a female driver and conductor. There were few men to be seen but many pale-faced children who appeared quite friendly and pleased to see us. We saw a crowd of women waiting outside the butchers and bakers.

1 September. I started Spanish again, this time with a small class of six. I'm beginning at the beginning again because I learnt practically nothing from the other fellow; I notice that the pronunciation is totally different.

2 September. Very hot today and lots of tennis . . . The management of the canteen has passed from the hands of a private

contractor into those of an international committee of officers, which means that the two damsels who dispensed coffee etc. have disappeared, to the great grief of those interned heroes who have spent two years here, sitting gazing at them most of the time. For my part I am more concerned in the fate of two Dachsunds which our room has more or less adopted. Anthony and Antoinette is what they answer to. They have been trained to fraternize with the British and bark at the Boche.

13 September. Started rehearsing in a 'Ragtime Octette'. There is a variety show coming on next month and this is one of the items. The idea of me in an Octette is, considering my vocal capabilities, distinctly good, but fortunately for all concerned I believe that there will be no need for me to sing but merely act the buffoon. Anything is better than to allow oneself to become like some people who spend most of their days in bed and are quite beyond doing anything.

16 September. Today we got a piano into our room so that I can picture our being far from popular with our neighbours, but as the room on our right has either a melodeon or a gramophone going all day they can't say much. As was to be expected many fellows rolled in after evening *appell* and we made merry until after eleven at which hour I appealed to them to withdraw rather than risk the removal of the piano which they cheerfully did.

5 October. I attended the Berlitz Spanish class and derived a certain amount of joy from it as the accent of the instructor differed from the two former ones . . .

18 October. One amusing incident – the inhabitants of Crefeld are rather given to taking their constitutionals in this direction and gazing at our windows as one would gaze at strange animals in the Zoo, while the small boys amuse themselves by singing various hymns of hate. This afternoon a large school of small girls put in an appearance, most of them in step, and singing *Deutschland uber alles* with much vigour, when suddenly they all

exploded, broke step, and turned in a second from a well-disciplined company to an unruly rabble. The cause of this was a fellow on the third floor who had donned a pierrot's hat, seized a wand, and proceeded to conduct from his window.

23 October. The first night of the show and apparently I made the other artists laugh too much as I was told that I must only spread myself at certain periods. The first night of all shows is for the orderlies and really acts as a final dress rehearsal. The whole thing went well. The first item was an orchestral selection, then a short sketch followed by a few cinematograph films, then a pipe selection played by three of us, followed by a foursome reel for which an orderly played. Then two recitations, a Dutch dance, a bottle and zylophone selection, and after the interval, our Octette.

W— at the piano, dressed as a girl, and the men, bar me, in white trousers, white dress coats with black facings, black waist-coats with white buttons, white gloves and white top hats: I exactly the reverse, being black where they were white and white where they were black, while I was made up *à la* George Robey. As luck would have it I sprained my ankle pretty badly in the reel but managed to go through with the Octette.

24 October. Can hardly walk today and spent most of my time with my foot in boiling water and being massaged by an orderly . . .

22 November. In the evening I went to the first night of the French theatre where I saw *Miquette et sa Mere*. It was absolutely up to first class London form both as regards acting and scenery; nothing could have been better. Somehow the French always appear to make better women than the other nations. The British come a good last!

27 November. There is a club here called 'The Apostles' Club' consisting of twelve members. One of these has gone and I have been elected to the vacant place which pleases me muchly . . .

30 November. St Andrew's Day and one of great excitement among the Scotch here. The Scots Guards officers gave a dinner at night at which there were eighteen of us. F— and I played in the Haggis and gave one or two selections after dinner and at the end of *appell* played Colonel B. off parade, after which we adjourned to his room where we had *Whisky*, spelt with a capital 'W'; this unaccustomed drink had the result of considerably cheering up many of the lads and we marched round the square with the pipes gathering people as we went until on reaching our room there was a nice little band of thirty-three all willing in case of need to be temporary Scots, particularly a Russian and a Frenchman who were both decked out in Glengarries.

3 December. The chief event was my initiation into the Apostles' Club, which was not nearly so terrifying as I had anticipated. There are various advantages in being a member, and not the least of these is that we have the private room every Sunday where one may sit and talk or write and on that evening most of the members usually dine there.

8 December. Great event today. I went into town shopping with Col B—, C— and N—. We were accompanied by an interpreter and had more than three hours there. We visited quite a number of shops likely to contain things useful for theatricals. The biggest shop we went to was a sort of baby Harrods and there we had quite an amusing time. Naturally we were stared at a good deal but there were more smiles than scowls and all the young ladies appeared to be distinctly friendly.

9 December. R— and I went down town to visit a hair specialist, in hope of saving our few remaining locks. On these jaunts one hands in a parole card and is accompanied by an unarmed guard. We spent about an hour in the waiting room where we saw and beamed upon quite a variety of humanity, and owing to a door being left open had an excellent view of a young lady having her golden tresses attended to. We then

interviewed the doctor who proved to be a cheery old bird and spoke a mixture of English and French. Being completely bald himself he was no great advertisement for his own cure! He told us that he had a son in England who was taken on the Somme and was being excellently treated and fed.

We were taken in hand by a buxom nurse with red hair and, having been given green goggles, were placed side by side under an apparatus which proceeded to give us an extremely strong sun-bath. We were supposed to stop there for five minutes but were so taken up with a young lady stretched on a couch undergoing Rontgen Ray treatment that we lost count of time and remained underneath the rays for fifteen minutes with the result that both our heads are a lurid pink today. The nurse explained in a loud voice that the lady was having spots removed from her face, which was quite amusing for us but must have been very embarrassing for her.

12 December. The first performance of *Within the Law*, in which I take the part of English Eddie. It is generally agreed that it beats the last French show, which I would not have thought possible. The principal girl was simply wonderful.

20 December. Went to the hair specialist and had my head heavily burned by the rays . . .

25 December. Xmas in captivity and for a crowd of down-trodden mortals we made merry right well. Most people had dinner parties at night, and after *appell* the world at large started visiting each other in any room that took their fancy, and the fun waxed fast and furious. The Germans turned out a guard of great strength and some fellows, more unfortunate than the rest, were removed to jug. There was nobody actually killed, although when two processions going in different directions met on the staircase there appeared to be every reason why there should be.

27 December. The first night of the Pantomime, *Dick Whittington,* in which I play the Alderman. It exceeded all expectations

and was received by an uproarious audience who joined in the choruses with immense vigour, people in the 5th row couldn't hear the band, while the even more cheery lads at the back of the house helped the pandemonium by smashing windows . . .

31 December . . . On the stroke of midnight the majority of the British gathered in the square to sing *Auld Lang Syne*, and after deafening cheers we all marched round three times, headed by the pipes and all howling different Scotch songs at once, stopping at the end of each lap to sing *Auld Lang Syne* again. A gentleman who was seeing in the New Year in prison states that the noise must have been heard half across the town.

1917 brought the coldest weather in living memory, and opportunity for the Crefeld Camp officers to add winter sports to their programme, with ice hockey and skating on rinks improvised on the tennis courts. It also brought rumblings of unrest from the local populace.

It was not so much the occasional sounds of revelry by night that disturbed them. When they gazed up at the windows of the camp, 'as at strange animals at the Zoo', while their sons sang hymns of hate, it was out of more than curiosity. What angered them was that these caged inmates were being a great deal better fed and clothed than they were.

Throughout Germany shortages of food, clothing and other commodities were becoming increasingly dire. And to the women noted by Lyall Grant queueing outside the butchers and bakers with their pale-faced children there was something all wrong about the sight of stacks of food parcels from England being unloaded at the station *en route* to the enemies of the Fatherland.

Another PoW's account of Crefeld at this time substantiates an incredible state of affairs hinted at by Lyall Grant towards the end of his stay. So bitter did local feeling become that there was a real threat of a hungry populace breaking into the camp (from which every inmate longed to get out) to raid those bountiful stores of goodies.

4 May. A quiet day until the evening, when some excitement was caused by the sudden arrival of a company of 'Active troops' heavily helmeted, and the doubling of the guard . . .

5 May. The double guard is still on, but no one can discover the reason. There is the usual rumour that the populace, feeling hungry, had had a demonstration and decided to come up and relieve us of our food. Fellows who have been down the town say that they are as friendly as ever . . .

7 May. The double guard is still on and there are now two machine guns in the fields outside and two on the roof of the buildings, but who they are afraid of we cannot yet make out. Of course we should like the populace to make a raid on our food store as there would always be the chance of getting out with them in the mêlée . . .

Two weeks later the camp was broken up, the inmates being split into four parties and sent to other camps. 'The Commandant gave no particular reason but said that he would be sorry to lose us,' Lyall Grant notes. The generally accepted reason was that it was because there had been an increase in attempted escapes. On 30 April there had been the most intensive search yet of the camp, when officers were stripped and their personal belongings as well as their quarters searched.

The search was conducted by the civil authorities as well as Army officers and guards. Had Lyall Grant's diary been found an entry of some weeks before would have been of particular interest to the civilian searchers, hinting as it does that the English officers were enjoying not only their Red Cross and personal parcels from home but the delicacies of a local black market.

Still freezing hard, and my only excitement was a dinner that I gave to some of the lads. The thing appeared to be a success and one great jest was when a haggis (as I thought) turned out to be a plum pudding. The menu was: Asparagus Soup; Sole; Duck or Goose with potatoes & greens; Plum Pudding; Sardines on

Toast; Coffee. So it's still possible to obtain some food in Germany. Most of it is smuggled over the Dutch border, and charged for accordingly.

The night before their departure on 20 May, the British contingent gave the burghers of Crefeld something more to brood over.

As soon as it got dark bonfires began to spring up all over the square, chairs, tennis nets etc. (all our private property which we could not move) being used as fuel. The Boche quite lost their heads, multitudinous guards were rushed in and the battalion (!) that had come to see us safely off surrounded the camp in addition to the extra cordon already there.

On the whole it was quite a rag and passed the time well. There were moments when one expected some excited worm to shoot, but none did although one took to hitting about with the butt of his rifle and landed Col B. a blow in the back when of course he was doing nothing. For this he was run in before the Commandant and I hope duly strafed.

Our room had a combined supper and breakfast, when we put all our crockery etc. (and there was a lot of it) on the table and threw the whole outfit out of the window. Unfortunately it missed the sentry below, but it made a beautiful noise . . .

The next five months were the closest Lyall Grant came to experiencing any real discomforts, though not remotely comparable to the ordeals of the Tommy. How wide was the gulf is indicated in a diary entry concerning the train trip from Crefeld to the new camp. One has only to recall accounts by other rank PoWs of nightmare journeys in crowded cattle trucks to find a faint air of the absurd in Lyall Grant's outrage:

The day was very hot and passed with a little sleep, reading and cards. We had our own food with us and as the two guards in the compartment had only one slice of bread and an egg for the day's ration we gave them some, much to their delight, but no water could be obtained at any price. Fortunately we had tea and lemons of our own, but that does not excuse the Germans for sending us for a 24-hours trip in a 2nd class carriage with no lavatory and giving us no water *en route*. When one thinks of the outcry there would be if German prisoners in England were treated like that it makes one sick . . .

Worse was to come. At 4 am on 23 May the British contingent disentrained at a halt called Schwarmstedt to be told that they had a three hours' march before them. 'The march turned out to be about 7 kilometres along sandy roads with marshes on either side,' writes Lyall Grant, 'and when we saw the camp we nearly threw a fit.'

Schwarmstedt Camp, in thickly wooded, marshy countryside some forty miles north of Hanover, made Crefeld seem like a palace. The sleeping and living quarters for 480 officers were four long wooden huts in a 4-acre clearing ringed by barbed wire, with three pumps in the middle providing drinking water and troughs to wash in. The dormitory huts were partitioned into rooms for ten, with no room for even a small table between the straw-mattressed beds. 'The walls are of planks by no means tight fitting—and this is where our enemies think fit to lodge British Officer PoWs!' exclaims Lyall Grant. On further investigation the gloom deepens.

We have had wine cards issued to us, but there is no wine. The afternoon of the first day was chiefly spent drinking a curious mixture going by the name of Lemonade, for which we stood in a long queue, drawing bread on a bread card which meant another queue of some fifty minutes with half a loaf at the end of it—that being our weekly ration, and airing our blankets, as several fellows found that a reception had been prepared for us by more than the Commandant . . .

The Commandant quite refuses to believe that we receive the

number of parcels that we say we do, and even the word of the Interpreter who came with us fails to convince him. Seeing is believing, so if they ever do arrive – which I doubt – he will have the shock of his life.

The very first night three officers managed to cut the wire and get away into the woods and marshes, though the Dutch border was now over a hundred miles away. A number of escape bids are recorded in the diary, most of them unsuccessful, and in one of which a Captain was shot dead by a camp guard, to be buried with full military honours (the Germans providing the firing party). But for Lyall Grant, once the food parcels and mail from home began to arrive, the Spanish lessons had been resumed and the need for exercise been reaffirmed by an expanding waistline, there was enough to do to make even Schwarmstedt bearable.

1 June. In the morning I washed all my dirty clothes, shorts, pyjamas, underthings etc. – quite an effort. We will become quite domesticated if we stop here long enough – which God forbid! The washing was done in a horse trough in the middle of the camp and the water is cold, but the weather being warm that doesn't matter so much . . .

2 June. No event of great importance today, except that I ran a mile and a quarter for a bet, and although winning nearly died in the attempt . . .

5 June. Re-started Shorthand and Spanish today, both with new tutors. The Boche ran all our room in on the charge of having a candle burning after 'lights out' on Sunday and laughing at the sentry when he told us to extinguish it. Pages of statements were taken from each of us which all worked out to the same thing, viz. guilty on the first charge, not guilty on the second. Incidentally we demanded to be confronted with the sentry to make him prove his accusation. This was refused, but the excitement that they made might have led one to think that we had killed the

fellow. Perhaps if we had there wouldn't have been so much panic as he could not have imagined that his dignity had been offended.

6 June. The Commandant fell our room in in front of him at morning *appell* and said that he believed our statement about not laughing at the sentry but that we had been very disorderly laughing among ourselves, also that we had had a candle burning, and therefore we would be confined to the Camp for three days. It does not appear to be funny in writing, but the formality of the whole thing was immense and the whole parade was highly entertained, ourselves included.

In the forenoon I spent quite a time in a queue to get my monthly pay. I then spent half an hour waiting to buy my weekly half loaf of bread. After the war, I picture all the fellows who have been here diving into any queue that they may see without even enquiring what it is there for.

9 June. I am now making strenuous efforts to reduce my ever-growing figure by means of two lots of physical drill daily . . . In the morning the Germans had a strenuous search for maps. It would have been a pity if all their energy had been expended in vain but in this case it was rewarded. They found two. One of the London Underground Railways and one of Tibet.

14 June. Went out on a parole walk in the woods again this morning and did a little piping. Met several 'Tommies' from a man's camp near here. They are all very cheery despite rotten conditions and have no respect for their guards whatever.

21 June. The anniversary of my wedding was evidently known by my hosts as some wine came in today. Extraordinarily bad, and the ration only one mug, but it sufficed to drink a silent toast.

10 July. A representative of the Dutch Embassy rolled up this morning and was shown round. All our complaints were put before him. Apparently he got instructions from Holland on 18 June to visit us so presumably some news had got home by

then. This reminds me that a couple of days ago we heard that three British officers had crossed the border and as two have been away from here for over a fortnight we hope that they may be of the three. If so people at home should hear interesting details before long . . .

14 July. A great day, being the Sports Day proper. The Padre won most of the over 30 years of age events. The Obstacle race was the last of the day, and very hard. Among other things the competitors had to go through two stagnant pools in the middle of the ground and the smell put up defies description. Quite the best day I've had for a long time—which isn't saying much, but there you are.

24 July. Played my Monthly Medal round on our new golf course . . .

1 August. Immense entertainment on this morning's *appell* as the Germans have now introduced a rule by which as we answer our names we take two paces to the right and this of course gave each room an opportunity to outdo the others with some comic movement. We are really rather like infants or lunatics, but then we get such extraordinary orders that they ask for ragging . . .

30 August. The latest idea of the Germans is to take a certain number of our personal orderlies and work them in the fields, among them our room orderly, so I suppose we'll be more uncomfortable than ever . . .

6 September. Quite an event today was the start of RUGGER. The ground can hardly be called suitable, being only 50 yards long and 25 yards wide, while a pump and an electric light pole are obstacles to be avoided. However, we had a good enough game with eleven a side and got hot, dirty and scraped.

13 September. The chief event was a concert at night in the dining hut. It was quite good, with some amusing topical songs and at the end we took off a very heavy melodrama in a sketch lasting about 15 minutes. I was the wicked squire, described as

'libertine, roué and gambler'. Everyone says that it was very funny.

16 September. Rumour has it that this camp will be closed at the end of next week.

It was with hopes high that the British officers entrained on 26 September, 1917, for their new camp. Lyall Grant was evidently in top form. 'I appeared to cause the Hun officers considerable annoyance by wearing a black-rimmed eyeglass attached to a huge piece of black tape and fixing them with a glassy stare whenever they addressed me.' He found this journey 'quite comfortable', in a 2nd class compartment with seven of his room-mates and a friendly guard who spoke bad French and who, on hearing that Lyall Grant was a Scot, asked if he could speak or understand English.

Their destination was the picturesque red-roofed town of Holzminden on the banks of the River Weser some fifty miles south of Hanover. As they neared the station they saw men waving from the windows of the massive four-storey barracks that constituted the camp. It was not the welcome it seemed.

From the train the barracks had looked very good, but our hopes were dashed when after a two-kilometre walk, dragging our hand luggage with us or leaving it on the road if it proved too heavy, we were greeted by many people shouting from the windows that it was the worst camp they had struck and telling us to look out for a personal search of the most rigorous nature.

At the end of the war Holzminden was to become famous as the scene of the most audacious tunnel escape from a top-security prison ever carried out, and for the iron-fisted régime of the most hated of all officer Camp Commandants, Karl Niemeyer. The 60 yards long tunnel (prototype of the more celebrated tunnels of World War II) was excavated over a period of nine months with spoons, penknives and a breadknife by the light of electric torches. On 23 July, 1918, twenty-nine British officers crawled out one by one beyond the high walls and barbed wire, ten of them eventually reaching the Dutch border and freedom. The brilliant escape was a death-blow to the self-esteem of Karl Niemeyer, who is believed to have committed suicide after the camp was liberated.

The British Press (turning a blind eye on the camps for other rank PoWs) dubbed Holzminden 'the worst camp in Germany', 'the German black hole', and clamoured for the trial of the 'Hun brute' who ran it. In a headlined picture-story of the camp's liberation, the *Daily Sketch* declared: 'At Holzminden the unfortunate captives lived under the most insanitary conditions, had to be content with starvation diet, were seldom visited by doctors, and at all times were the victims of brutal treatment.'

Lyall Grant's diary account of six months in this 'black hole' is a good deal less sensational. His chief complaints are the petty and humiliating regulations and restrictions (with spells in the cells for offenders), the absence of many of the amenities taken for granted at Crefeld, the chivvying of guards, and blatant profiteering in the canteen, particularly in wine. Niemeyer comes over more as an arrogant buffoon than a brute.

The question remains, however, how much Lyall Grant left out in his diary entries for fear of reprisals. In a footnote to one entry, added after the war, he writes:

Some things I could not put in the Diary for fear it might be discovered. When we got to Holzminden we found a regular 'Escape Committee' in being. They owned a sewing machine and were expert thieves. They made up German kits for would-be escapers, and rigged them out. By a very ingenious device they had filed the bolts of a door at the end of the building so that, although these appeared to be in position, the door could be opened. By this way the escapers went through the Commandant's private house and through the gate in twos or threes, the sentry taking them for Huns carrying sacks of rubbish, whereas the sacks really contained civilian clothing and food. The scheme was discovered the night before G. and I were booked to do an exit.

This is the only intimation that Lyall Grant had ever himself contemplated escape. But that he makes no mention in a footnote of the tunnelling that started shortly after his arrival, suggests that he was not personally interested in a long-term project. As numerous references in this section of the diary indicate, all his hopes were now centred on the possibility of repatriation. For some months the belligerent powers had been negotiating a scheme for the exchange of prisoners, to be accommodated in neutral countries until the end of the war, eligibility depending on date of capture. For long-serving prisoners like Lyall Grant anything that might jeopardize their inclusion on the list was to be avoided.

Whether the possibility of his diary being discovered led him to tone down his references to the 'Hun brute' Niemeyer, or whether he was merely more thick-skinned than most, is also conjectural. In other accounts of Holzminden (notably the 1920 best-seller *The Tunnellers of Holzminden*, written by one of the escapees), he emerges as an offensive tyrant, dedicated to humiliating and breaking the spirit of his officer prisoners, and loathed almost as much by the German camp staff as by the British.

With his equally hated twin brother Heinrick, who was Commandant at Clausthal Camp, Karl had spent seventeen years before the war in Milwaukee, USA, and spoke English in what was described as 'bartender Yank'. He was fluent but given to ludicrous errors of speech. Particularly cherished by the inmates of Holzminden was his tirade at a group of prisoners suspected of plotting to escape: 'You think, gentlemen, I know nothing of your little plans, but I tell you I know damn all.'

Mockery had long been recognized by Lyall Grant as the most effective weapon against the humourless Hun. Seven weeks after his arrival at Holzminden he scored a bull's-eye, his victim the tyrannous Niemeyer. Until then the diary has few, but revealing, references to him:

The old hands tell us that the Commandant, by name Niemeyer, is most antagonistic and does everything to make life as uncomfortable as possible . . .

At the moment the cells are full. Anyone requiring a rest has only to pass the Commandant without saluting and he gets what he is looking for . . .

The Commandant caused a fair amount of amusement by raving round. He is followed by a crowd watching for any fun that he may provide . . .

One fellow who had waited for two hours in the queue for parcels mentioned the fact to the Commandant as he passed and received the reply that he didn't care a damn if he waited ten hours! . . .

This morning the Commandant stopped all orderlies' tins for a week because he considered that they were working badly, so now of course we are looking after them as well as ourselves. Probably *his* chief effort of the day was to walk into a room and expectorate on the floor . . .

Of the incident that led up to Lyall Grant's brief but highly satisfactory confrontation with the Commandant there is regrettably no account in the diary.

5 November. I am writing this in jug, where I have retired for three days' rest for doing the goose step on *appell.* My cell is simply a cellar, about 8′ high, 6′ broad and 15′ long, with one small window up at the ground level. It is very cold but I get a stove lit in the afternoon so am really better off here than outside.

By shouting I can talk to the two fellows next door on either side. As I brought my own mattress I am quite comfortable in bed and stop there most of the day. The other furniture is a table, stool, tin basin and jug.

9 November . . . Had an interview with the Commandant on the subject of my imprisonment for doing what he called a 'comic walk'. I pointed out that some people were born with

stammers and some with peculiar walks and I was one of the latter. He said that, that being so, he would tell his Officers that I could walk as I liked on *appell.* Truly the Hun has no sense of humour.

During the rest of his captivity the light at the end of the tunnel for Lyall Grant was neutral Holland—to be reached legitimately as a reward for 'long service' as a PoW. Of the other way of reaching it, via the actual tunnel in process of excavation under the very nose of Niemeyer, there is not a hint, though references are made to individual attempts at escape. For Lyall Grant, as for most of Holzminden's 500 officer prisoners, it was the same old round of games, theatricals and very occasional festivity, in which the price and quality of the wine becomes a burning issue, and an outing to an oculist a memorable occasion.

10 November. Hockey has started but the ground is too small and the ball spends most of its time between the inner and outer wire, in the neutral zone as it is called, where one would get shot at for going in pursuit of it.

22 November. Cold and wet, but excellent news from the West Front. We are to have a concert in this house on the 24th, finishing with a sketch called *The Artist's Model.* I am to be the model . . .

24 November. The concert passed off well and the sketch was quite a good show. I fancy I must have looked rather sweet as the 'Model', in a small ballet frock and tights, with a wreath on my head.

27 November. Three of us went today to a place called Brackle to see an oculist. It was just over an hour by train and made a pleasant outing, particularly as after the interview we lunched at the village pub and it was a treat to get something that didn't come out of a tin. Menu as follows:—Vegetable soup, hare with potatoes and vegetables, gooseberries and milk, cheese and bread (no butter available), all washed down by Château Laon.

We left here at 8 am and got back at 6 pm. The people we met were all quite friendly but there was a little trouble at the far end because we travelled 2nd class whereas the stationmaster said we should have been 3rd. I went armed with an enormous dictionary and used it freely, which caused much amusement. The guard who went with us had rather a heavy day. Going there our train had to wait half an hour at a junction and we insisted on getting out and visiting the refreshment room, with the result that when the other train came in we were missing and they had to keep our train waiting until they found us.

At lunch when we wished to order more wine the guard refused on the ground that the money given to him to pay expenses was finished and, as we had only camp money (issued for use in Camp and no good outside), nothing could be done. We rather surprised him by producing 180 marks of *real* money and so were able to get on with the good work, with the result that on the homeward journey we had to do the guide, philosopher and friend act on him.

28 November. Went to the Camp dentist today and had a couple of teeth stopped. He seemed to be quite good but not too gentle. Throughout his performance he wore his sword which amused me.

30 November. St Andrew's Day, and passed off quite well. At night there were parties in each house and we had the pipes going in ours. Of course it didn't come up to the show at Crefeld, but I didn't think we could have made so much row here without someone being shot.

2 December. Heavy driving snow and sleet and bitterly cold, also no fuel to warm us up. The rash has broken out on my face again, quite a number of fellows have it. It is probably caused by eating nothing but tinned food and is certainly very uncomfortable.

16 January, 1918. It is over a month since I wrote anything in

this diary. This was caused by our hearing that when we left this country *all* written matter would be taken off us. Now we hear that the first two parties for Holland were hardly searched at all, so I'll start again . . .

An event worthy of mention was the departure of Commander B. for another camp early in December. It so happened that a couple of nights before a fellow had tried to escape by sliding from a window over the top of the wire on a slide made of shelves from the dining-room, and the Commandant had ordered the dining-room doors to be locked in consequence.

A general 'strafe' for an attempted escape is absolutely illegal. The doors were of course broken down and next day all our houses were confined to their rooms until those who broke the doors owned up, which they were ordered not to do. By this time Commander B. had made his presence too warm for the Commandant, so he was given two hours to pack and was cleared off amid a great ovation, our house cheering him from the windows and 'A' house seeing him off at the gate. We were liberated the same night as 'A' house had tabooed the canteen, and as the Commandant gets the profit on the wine that hit too near home. I think I have already mentioned that wine costs 11 or 12 marks a bottle, while its real value is more like 3 . . .

On Christmas Day no sale of wine was allowed so we showed our appreciation by making sufficient noise to be heard in the town, and got the wine shut off for two more days. Incidentally, most people had laid in a stock beforehand. Our room gave a party which was a great success. A party here costs just about ten times as much as it would at the Carlton, but they are few and far between and supply a topic of conversation for some time.

On Hogmanay we had the usual midnight procession with the pipes, and for once the Germans behaved sensibly—in other words kept out of our way . . .

Theatricals have had a boom but things can't be done on the Crefeld scale. However, quite a big stage is made out of tables at the end of the dining-room and there are plenty of experts for scenery and lighting . . .

The only other thing of interest to bring the diary up-to-date is that yesterday one G., of the West Yorks, held a Royal Straight Flush, the first I have met.

4 February. The following is a copy of a very interesting document on the subject of wine which has been put up on the board:

'WINE.

The whole question of WINE in this camp is nothing less than a SCANDAL. The wine is sold unnamed and the quality is abominable. If the bottles are held up to the light the wine will be found (with a few exceptions) to be *clouded*, that is to say it has gone wrong. No good (or even bad or indifferent) wine merchant would dare to sell wine thus "clouded". It would be poured down the sink. In other words the canteen wine is quite *unmarketable* in the Wine Trade. It cannot be claimed that this is new wine which has not had time to settle as, if the corks are examined, many will be found covered with mildew, at least two years old . . .'

The lengthy notice, directly aimed at the profiteering Commandant, includes a selection of prices from a 1915 Army & Navy Stores Wine List, and concludes that, over a three-month period and on an estimated daily sale of 100 bottles, 'someone—one knows not whom—has pocketed *Mks 36,000* on 9,200 bottles'. It demanded that the canteen price per bottle be reduced from 11 to 6·50 marks. A boycott of the canteen eventually led to some concessions.

6 February . . . The great rumour today is that the British are

starting a Ladies' Flying Corps, and the selfish ones here hope that the Germans will take many of them prisoners and send them along here.

8 February. The theatre was a great success and I am glad to say our potted version of *The Touch of the Child* was immense, the place rocked with joy.

10 February. We had quite an exciting quarter of an hour this afternoon. Two fellows M. and W. put up an extraordinarily stout show by getting across the 'neutral zone' while the sentries' backs were turned for a moment, cutting the wire on the top of the railings, pulling themselves up and dropping over. They then started to walk up the road but, by a stroke of bad luck, they were spotted by a German looking out of a cellar window who gave the alarm and assisted in hoisting a sentry over the fence after them. He fired one shot and started in pursuit, followed by most of the rest of the garrison and numerous dogs and small boys. The fugitives displayed great staying powers and out-distanced their pursuers, watched by an interested mob from all the windows, but luck was against them and the appearance of a man from a sentry box put an end to their attempt . . .

11 February. I have now started rehearsing for a dramatic sketch entitled *Unchartered Waters*, in which I am doing the heavy . . . We have also started a Reel Club which should provide quite a lot of exercise.

16 February . . . I refereed a Rugger match under the old Schwarmstedt rules—Infantry v The World. The former won after a very good game . . .

28 February. The last day of another month and Holland appears to be no nearer and the end of the war further away. What a life! My leg is still bad and will be until I can get plenty of vegetables.

3 March. Very busy rehearsing for *Laughter in Court* . . .

8 March. A beautiful day and as soccer has been allowed again

I spent some time watching a game. The ground is so small that several local rules are necessary.

9 March. Heard from some of our interned friends in Holland today. Everyone seems very pleased with the comparative freedom, but all agree that Holland is most expensive. The fashionable thing seems to be to spend all your money in about three days and then retire to a sanatorium.

17 March. St Patrick's Day was duly celebrated by the Irish with a luncheon, but I fancy that it must have grieved the Patron Saint to see his followers sitting down to a teetotal feast. In the evening seven of us had a small dinner during which we also were Irish and perhaps not quite so dry as the real ones, considerable thought having been given to the subject and brandy procured in exchange for soap.

20 March. A cricket net has been put up, but there is no matting and it is quite impossible to make anything like a true pitch, so the game is more dangerous than amusing.

23 March. We heard of the start of the German offensive in the West and our hosts were very uppish on the result of the first day . . .

24 March. The news from the West Front not too good, but we only hear the German side. One of the German officers showed excellent taste by remarking to our orderlies, 'England Kaput!' Fancy a British officer making a remark like that to German soldiers!

25 March. News about the West Front not very cheering . . . On evening *appell* an officer waved a special evening edition to us and then pinned it on the notice board. Needless to say it told of the taking of Bapaume and another 15,000 prisoners. However, he who laughs last laughs longest.

28 March. The Germans appear to be slowing down a bit and I hope are nearly stopped . . .

1 April. The day began in an appropriate manner by a fellow in

'A' house giving their Adjutant some animals' teeth that looked rather human and saying that he had found them in the bath-house. So when the Adjutant gave out on *appell* that a set of false teeth had been found, two people who were in the know marched out and gave a very exaggerated salute—which led to a great scene as the German officer thought they were taking off the German salute and raved wildly, to the great delight of the onlookers . . .

6 April. My birthday. I must say I didn't expect to see another in Germany but have no doubt now that the War will be going on this time a year hence.

The Pierrot show was given in 'B' house and went splendidly; all the latest ragtimes and several songs with topical verses. I was included in the cast, by way of lending a comic element. The second scene is a very good one, being a night scene with Chinese lanterns, a lighted casino and pier, and the waves moving in the moonlight . . .

18 April. The chief amusement today was a baseball match between the winners of the Baseball League (mostly Canadians) and 'B' house 'Mugs', a team who knew little about baseball but something about cricket. I performed for the 'Mugs' and to the great amusement of the crowd we won!

19 April. Primrose Day, but no primroses.

22 April. Truly a great day. The canteen 'strafe' was taken off and my name appeared on the Holland list. The latter was rather an expensive business as I had bet that I would not leave before May.

23–25 April. Occupied with packing and preparations for departure. The greater part of my diary was sewn in the waist-band of my kilt by a Gordon Highlander, one of our Orderlies, the remainder went inside the bag of my pipes. I also packed some small notes from other people—to be posted home from Holland—inside the back of a hairbrush prepared for the purpose . . .

26 April. We were thoroughly searched but I managed to get quite a lot of prison coins through, which will make good souvenirs and do for tips to German waiters if I am ever unfortunate enough to meet any.

We fell in at 8 am and were cheered as we came away by those left behind. We had a final scowl at the Commandant who was trying to be friendly, and no one shook hands with him. We travelled 2nd class, reaching Aachen about 10 pm.

29 April. On arrival at Aachen we were marched to a school, where we were kept for three days, with nothing to do, but quite well fed. Here we met parties from various other camps and no Mothers' Meeting ever talked as we did—the usually stolid Briton was quite off his head with excitement.

We were again searched, especially for hidden diaries, being told that if anyone had one and gave it up nothing would be said, but that if any were found in the search the owners would be sent back to Germany and kept there until the end of the war. I thought this was probably bluff and, as my diary was well hidden, I decided to risk it. All was well, but I spent a very uncomfortable half hour, especially when a searcher pawed all round my waist.

During our stay at Aachen the Huns tried to be very friendly, but we would have nothing to do with them.

30 April. We left Aachen about 7 am and got to Venloo on the Dutch frontier early in the afternoon; overjoyed at the sight of the first Dutch sentry.

There we had a great reception, were given coffee and cakes, and got into a most luxurious train, leaving our German guards to return to the Fatherland and empty tummies.

In the train we got English newspapers, chocolates and cigarettes, and had dinner on arrival at Rotterdam. We reached The Hague at 10 pm and walked from the station through lines of troops and cheering inhabitants while our friends beat us black and blue.

The official reception took place in a café, where there were speeches, cheers, tea and cakes. When this was over we were seized by friends and borne off to various entertainments. A lot of us were taken to Daly's Night Club where we got a tremendous welcome, and pandemonium reigned until the place closed at midnight, when we went to our hotels and about twenty of us sat down to a meal which lasted until 4 am.

At the end of the typescript copy of his diary, Lyall Grant has written in ink: 'In one sketch that I played in I had to repeat some lines of Shelley's which will make a fitting end to this Diary—viz "The World's great age begins anew, the Golden Years return".'

For him the years ahead were not entirely golden. His first wife died in 1920, his dearly loved eldest son was killed in the Second World War. He worked all his life for a living, in turn as a Merchant Banker, a paint salesman, and (until the time of his death) a whisky salesman. During the Second World War he saw plenty of action as Officer-in-Command of a troopship at the Sicily landings and elsewhere.

But to his friends he was always the 'gay cavalier', living exuberantly in the present. And it is perhaps scarcely surprising that the diary he had once so resolutely kept and so cunningly concealed was as readily forgotten.

The *London Scottish Regimental Gazette* for August, 1920, carried this note about him: 'He went to France in 1914 and served with distinction, eventually being appointed one of the landing officers at Boulogne. He sojourned for a time with brother Boche, an account of which sojourn is a little overdue for the *Gazette*.'

No account was forthcoming and no one can now recall any mention of the diary. It is thought likely that he destroyed the original diary notebooks, and sent the typescript copy to the War Office (who passed it on to the Imperial War Museum), when clearing out his Wimbledon home after the death of his second wife, prior to moving to the private hotel where he lived for the last seven years of his life.

'He was a great "caster-out"—people were more important to him than possessions,' says Mrs Susan Benfield, youngest of five children by his two marriages. 'He was an immensely active person, always on the move, looking at his watch, jiggling the coins in his pocket. One can imagine how he must have hated being cooped up as a prisoner. On reading his diary for the first time, I find it remarkable how he managed to view his time as a PoW in such a light-hearted manner. And it should not be thought that he was just someone who went through life always in a jocular frame of mind, rushing from one party to another! He had a serious side to his nature, was a great reader and a devoted family man.'

Four photographs taken at different times of his life hint at the 'panache' remembered by his friends. Aged 18, he is the conspicuously debonair member of Glenalmond Cricket XI, sporting an embryo moustache. Aged 29, in the Crefeld Camp 'Octette', he dominates the stage in white top hat and blazer, leaning languidly on his cane while a bewigged 'girl', in short white dress and white stockings, ogles up at him.

Aged 76, a stocky bespectacled figure in bowler hat and medal-bedecked lounge suit, he escorts the Queen Mother down the ranks of the veterans at a Jubilee parade of the London Scottish Old Comrades Association, of which, like his father before him, he was Chairman. Aged 78, ringed by a grinning group of Territorials, he is the life and soul of the party, face puckered in mirth under a balding dome, bagpipes at the ready.

Lyall Grant joined the London Scottish as a humble piper and finished up as Commanding Officer. And, apart from the London Scottish Rugby Football Club, of which he was President, it was at the Regimental Headquarters near Buckingham Palace that he was most in his element. There the memory of him lives on. Memories of his sporting prowess, of his after-dinner speeches that set the table aroar, of the bagpipe parades and horseplay as the drink flowed. It seems no great remove from Gütersloh and Crefeld.

'He was always a boy at heart,' reflected one Old Comrade at the monthly get-together in the bar he never failed to attend. 'He died as he would have wished, suddenly, after a night out with the lads. After a cricket club dinner at Wimbledon, he waved goodbye to his friends, set off to walk home to his private hotel, and round the corner dropped dead from a heart attack.

'After nine years we still feel his presence. Any time he could come breezing in through that door and the fun would start.'

Chapter Five

JEEVES IN KHAKI

PRIVATE NORMAN DYKES

TAKEN FOR GRANTED by officer prisoners of war were the other rank orderlies who waited on them hand and foot, from making their beds and polishing their boots to preparing and serving their meals. Private Norman Dykes was at Crefeld and Schwarmstedt at the same time as Captain Lyall Grant, but from their two accounts of life there they could have been in separate worlds.

It was not only in rank but in temperament that they differed. An assistant at Rochdale Public Library before joining the Royal Fusiliers in November, 1915, Dykes was something of a loner, who made few close friends during his 2½ years captivity, played little part in camp entertainments (though a useful inside left on the soccer field), and rated as one of his happiest periods the formation and running of a library for other ranks.

Still active at 80, Dykes looks back on his First World War experiences, both in the trenches and in PoW camps, as a highlight (however harrowing at times) in his life. Among his most cherished possessions are the notebooks he kept throughout his captivity, later written up into a 100,000-word journal he entitled *All For A Shilling A Day!* and tried in vain to get published. It is from the notebooks and the journal that the extracts that follow have been taken.

It is significant that Lyall Grant, although the least snobbish and stand-offish of men, only once refers individually to an orderly (the Gordon Highlander who sewed his diaries into the waistband of his kilt on the eve of his release). In one entry he gives a presumably tongue-in-cheek 'list of rules that we have for our "weekly orderly", viz. the fellow whose turn it is to make early morning tea, etc.'

They range from 'It is to be remembered that he probably suffers from a weak heart and an enlarged spleen, therefore must be spoken to gently', to 'It is to be remembered that (1st) the orderly for the week is a man, and (2nd) that "All men are liars"—so perhaps he did not always *forget* to lay out various items on the table but hoped that they wouldn't be necessary.'

Lyall Grant's other references (apart from those included in the last chapter) are mostly concerned with Officers v Orderlies soccer matches, and with reciprocal visits to the entertainments provided on both sides of the social fence. Having in mind that the ratio of officers to orderlies was normally as high as five to one (100 orderlies at Holzminden for 500 officers), it is to be concluded that to him they were shadowy figures, part of the scenery, and that their activities were accepted much as a clubman might accept the comings and goings of stewards and waiters.

That Dykes for the most part accepted his menial role without resentment as being in the natural order of things is a measure of our changed society. Even today he is surprised that any special interest should be shown in this section of his journal. 'We had come to accept rank and privilege as a central factor of army life, but I suppose there was more to it than that,' he reflects. 'In civilian life we had taken for granted the bridge between the classes in a way that would not be tolerated now. "Upstairs–Downstairs" was a reality then, remember. Being an orderly meant that you were comfortably housed and well fed, and most officers were generous with "perks", both in payment and kind. So far as I was concerned, if an officer treated me as a human being I responded to him; if he treated me like dirt there were ways of getting back at him.'

Dykes was 18 when he was taken prisoner in the attack on High Wood on 20 July, 1916, three weeks after the launching of the Somme offensive. It was a nightmare experience that lingered with him in the cattle trucks that took the other-rank prisoners to Germany. The next five months were spent in three different camps (Dolmen, Rothe-nuffeln and Minden). He found the life harsh, monotonous and depressing (apart from a spell as librarian at Minden), and got in quickly when word went round that eight orderlies were wanted for

Gütersloh Camp (from which Lyall Grant had transferred four months before to Crefeld).

First impressions of Gütersloh were encouraging. 'There were many and lofty buildings with as many wide spaces between them; it was unlike any other camp I had been in or seen, and not like the doss-house type peopled by common-or-garden prisoners.'

For the 150 British officers languishing at Gütersloh there were thirty orderlies, employed not only as batmen and mess waiters but as maids-of-all-work, keeping their masters' quarters clean and in good repair. Before long Dykes and his seven Minden companions (including his husky Gordon Highlander 'mucking-in chum' McDonald) were knuckling down to the rigours of domestic service.

My lot was to take over the care of five officers in a room, and two in a much smaller compartment known as a 'bunk'. I was first introduced to the two officers in the 'bunk', Captains Randall and Clibborn, as their new servant, their regular servant having been despatched from the presence, having been guilty of some misdemeanour. They glanced at me without much enthusiasm; one remarked, 'I hope you will prove more satisfactory than your predecessor.' The ordeal was repeated when I was introduced to the remaining five of my flock: Captains Watson and Pirie, Lieut Duke, Naval Lieut Dolling-Smith, and 2nd Lieut Tilley.

My duties commenced at 7 am. My first charge was to supply early morning tea to Watson, Pirie and Duke. The teapot, complete with leaves and three cups and saucers, was left just inside the room on a tray on a table. Hot water was obtainable at the cookhouse between 6.30 and 8 every morning. I had to remember that Lieut Duke did not take sugar. After placing the three cups and saucers within easy reach of the appropriate officers' right hands, I had to collect the boots, shoes, tunics and hats of the five officers, clean and polish them as required, place them in the designated position as expounded by each individual officer, and withdraw quietly to serve the same purpose to the two officers in the bunk.

After morning parade, I had to make the beds of all seven officers, clean out their quarters and tidy, dust and straighten the articles in the room and bunk as needed. In addition, the orderlies on each floor were held jointly responsible for the sweeping, cleaning and dusting of the corridors and steps leading to and from them.

Seven o'clock on my first morning found me on my way from House 'A' to House 'B' with a determination to impress. I went along in the darkness with a feeling of nervousness, like the last man going in to bat, and the fast bowler glaring at me as I passed him on my way to the wicket. I groped my way to the room containing the five officers, cautiously opened the door, and with the good intention of not disturbing the slumbering inmates, attempted to locate the tray.

My idea of the geography of the place was admittedly hazy, but I think the gentleman with the large field boots might have put them a little more under his bunk. Still, he hadn't, and I sprawled over them, coming perilously near tipping the tray and its contents on the floor. The accompanying evolutions were not accomplished without noise, and in the midst of them a plaintive voice out of the darkness suggested that I might find it an advantage to switch on the light. This I eventually succeeded in doing after treading on more shoes and barking my shins against the side of a bunk. I could have sworn that the floor was positively strewn with boots and shoes, but they must have all jumped back under the bunks when the room was flooded with light.

I muttered an apology, made a grab for the teapot, cast a hurried glance round the room, noticed eyes here and there regarding me from the recesses of the beds, and beat a hasty retreat, leaving the light on in my haste to cover my confusion. I obtained hot water from the cookhouse and returned with my pot of tea to find the light still burning, and the eyes regarding me. The operation of pouring out the three cups of tea was accomplished unaccompanied by any untoward incident, the cups deposited where required, and I proceeded to get on with my next sphere of operations, collection of tunics and boots for cleaning.

Beyond dropping boots with a clatter on the hard floor of the passage, I completed the job with expedition, returning the articles to their several places in the room. The light was still on, so apparently the officers didn't mind it, or they were too comfortable to get out of bed to switch it off. All that remained now before being free to partake of my own breakfast was to perform a like service for the two captains in the bunk, who, so far, had been permitted to slumber without interference . . .

After morning parade we were dismissed to go and get on with our jobs of bedmaking, dusting and cleaning up. When I got to the room housing the five officers, I was informed by one of the two officers in the room that, apart from cleaning two pairs of boots belonging to one officer, leaving another with dirty footwear, and generally mixing up the boots and tunics, I had done well; I could feel my chest swelling with pride in my accomplishment!

When the other three officers sauntered into the room, I realized that five officers in one room was five too many when bed-making is the next operation. One cannot very well tell a superior in rank to move his carcass. With the use of a few 'Excuse me's' and 'I *am* so sorry', I at last managed to get all the beds made.

Next job was the rugs and carpets. I collected them and deposited them in the corridor outside. This was the sign for four of the five to set a course for the door. The fifth remained, reading a book. Not for long. Armed with a sweeping brush, I started a vigorous attack on the dusty floor. The last survivor beat a hasty retreat.

I was able to make progress now, dusting the chairs and the table, shaking the tablecloth, emptying the ashtrays, tidying and dusting the books, rinsing and cleaning the sink, emptying the dirty water in the waste bucket down the drain, filling the water jug. Next job, giving the rugs and carpets a good shaking and beating against the wall in the corridor and replacing them in the room. Then to the bunk, to give that room the same treatment.

It seemed to me a good job, well done; even to folding the pyjamas neatly and placing them in position on the beds. Finally, washing up the early morning cups, and storing them away in the cupboard. The last job was cleaning up in the corridor, then I was at liberty to return to my own room in House 'A': a room accommodating twenty orderlies in double-decker bunks ranged round the walls . . .

Dykes' afternoon was spent on 'fatigues' (packing waste paper into bundles for disposal), but there was one more batman's chore. 'Most officers seemed to indulge in afternoon tea, and they had it in their rooms, preparing it themselves, but the orderlies were expected to go along and clear up when the officers were in the dining-room at dinner.'

Apart from two occasions when he was 'carpeted', once for putting salt instead of sugar in the early morning tea, once for leaving a bed lumpy by not punching the mattress enough, Dykes found most of his officers pleasant and easy going.

As a rule a strong bond of friendship developed between the officers and the orderlies, and a genuine interest was taken in our welfare. An orderly need never be short of food or clothing (officers seemed to get unlimited supplies out from Britain). We were frequently asked about the condition of our wardrobe.

Sport was the nearest thing to common ground.

The very first evening of our arrival, we were buttonholed by an orderly who enquired hopefully and anxiously if there were any footballers amongst us. There was a match between the officers and orderlies on the following Sunday afternoon, and the orderlies were having some trouble in getting a full team together. Of course, the officers did not play their best team; they had a much wider choice than the orderlies to a ratio of five to one. If only we could wallop the team they selected, so that they had to choose a stronger team! Ewing and I, from the new arrivals, were chosen to turn out for the match on 7 January, 1917.

The pitch was of a sandy nature and kicked up rather during the game. We tried very hard – ran ourselves into the ground, as they say. They were too good for us, and won by two goals to one; I managed to score the orderlies' goal, playing at inside left. Our captain was very pleased, and picked the same team for the following Sunday. But we did not play again in Gütersloh. There was a heavy fall of snow during the week, and football was off.

The freezing weather brought sporting events that would have seemed beyond the wildest flights of fancy in an other ranks' PoW camp. Gütersloh far outdid the tennis court ice-rink at Crefeld that Lyall Grant was writing about at this time.

The officers soon hit upon a splendid idea. They set to work banking up the snow and rolling it flat on the hockey ground, approximately 60 yards by 20. The prepared area was flooded with water, and then left for nature to get to work on it. Soon as perfect a skating rink as could be desired was ready for the skaters, of which there were a goodly number in the camp. Great care was taken of the rink, and it was religiously brushed and reflooded at the end of each day of the seven weeks that the frost held . . .

Many thrilling games of ice hockey were enjoyed by players and spectators alike, and there were some marvellous exhibitions of trick and figure skating, mostly performed by Russian officers who seemed adept at this kind of thing. Orderlies were permitted to indulge at certain hours, and many availed themselves of the opportunity, some who hadn't worn skates ever before, I amongst them. Skates were very kindly lent to us, and we started off with any amount of encouragement from onlookers who were obviously expecting something to happen, and they were not disappointed.

I very soon discovered that ice was extremely hard, and I found it quite impossible to regain my feet once I was off them. I was finally compelled to make my way painfully and slowly, on hands and knees, to the edge of the rink, and although I was invited to give another demonstration, I declined with as much dignity as I could muster.

The skating season reached its peak when an Ice Carnival was organized at the beginning of March. The *pièce de résistance* was to be an ice hockey match between Russia on the one hand, who could field the strongest national team, and the British and French on the other. Refreshments were to be provided, and the British undertook to supply these. The Officers' Orchestra consented to provide musical interludes, and the fête bade fair to be one of the outstanding events in the annals of Gütersloh Prisoners of War Camp.

I, unfortunately, was not able to see much of the Carnival, having to turn out for scavenging work during the afternoon, and was only released in time to witness the concluding stages of the hockey match, and hear selections played by the orchestra, which had been esconced on the veranda to House 'D', an ideal position overlooking the rink. The effect of the music in the cold crisp air was wholly delightful. I was made envious by the description of the trick skating performed by two Russians and a Frenchman, and was disappointed that the hockey match should be virtually the end of the day's programme, that the orchestra should pack up and depart, and only a few enthusiasts remain to pursue their inclinations on the ice.

A harassing ten days spell as mess waiter in the dining-room at Gütersloh had convinced Dykes that he was better suited to the role of 'chamber maid'. How degrading that role could become at the hands of officer 'tartars' he was to find out at his next camp, Crefeld.

On the day he arrived at Crefeld, 21 March, 1917, Lyall Grant was recording in his diary: 'A day of immense excitement as the Russians went off amid much noise, and Gütersloh arrived en masse three hours later, when of course nothing was ready for them and the whole place was in a state of chaos, as all the old hands were in the act of bagging the best places and the corridors were packed with beds, boxes etc., while orderlies were hard at it cleaning up the rooms just left by the Russians . . . In the evening we put on the theatrical show for the Gütersloh crowd, to try to cheer them up, which I'm glad to say we did.'

The Gütersloh orderlies were dismally housed in converted stables attached to the cavalry barracks. Settled in, they were instructed to report to their new 'masters'. Dykes knocked with some foreboding on the door of Room 13 in Block K11. Five of the eight occupants were friendly young officers just arrived from Gütersloh. The other three, strangers from another camp, were 'rather repelling from their appearance and manner, prematurely aged, old womanly.'

Two days later the Gütersloh officers found more congenial room-mates elsewhere, and Dykes was in trouble:

Changes followed quite rapidly upon each other in K11–13, but always the three old fogies remained, and the worst elements seemed to be drawn to them, so that from discouragement my moods passed to depression, annoyance, detestation, covert disobedience, and thinly veiled insolence. I became thoroughly unhappy in my work, and purposely neglected my duties in the hope, which was finally realized, that I should be supplanted.

As an instance of the kind of treatment to which I was subjected by these officers, but not gentlemen, an officer in the Royal Naval Air Service took up residence. It was evident from the outset that this officer had been very badly spoiled in his upbringing and that he intended to have his every little wish gratified so far as service from the unfortunate orderly was concerned.

The morning following his arrival, he had me on the carpet, and, though he was not the senior officer in the room, he gave me to understand that I took my orders from him. His manner immediately roused my resentment, especially when hc said sharply, 'Stand to attention, Dykes, when you are being addressed by me.' My resentment must have been apparent to him, because he then snapped, 'I will not tolerate insolence from an orderly!'

I felt no pride in my native county of Lancashire when I learned that this was one of its products, and I could not help but think that for arrogance and selfishness this young man would run the most autocratic Prussian very closely. Without doubt he expected the same servility under prison camp conditions in Germany as had apparently been his portion when he had an orderly to himself.

After two days this officer produced a timetable, which must have employed his mind for some time, and which seemed intended to keep me employed the whole of my waking life at Crefeld. I felt myself getting hotter and hotter during the reading of my duties, which, incidentally, took place in the presence of the other members of the room, and had received their approbation, and at the end of the recital I was quite too full for words, could only accept the neatly constructed timetable and retire precipitately.

This timetable included cups of tea at 7 am, the daily cleaning of boots etc, my morning's work in the room, including scrubbing and swilling once weekly. All this particular officer's meals were to be served by me in the living room, and this meant taking the food to the cookhouse for heating or cooking, bringing it back to the room at a particular time, laying table, and all the other tasks incidental to the provision of a meal.

Many other tasks were enumerated, most of which decent officers would have performed themselves, and the more I studied the chart the more annoyed I became. I nearly decided to refuse point blank and take the consequences, which could only be my ignominious return to a men's camp and its unsavoury conditions. Then I thought it was worth while carrying on if only to derive some satisfaction by making these autocratic bullies pay for their complete lack of consideration.

My relations with the occupants of K11–13 gradually deteriorated, and though I never permitted myself to show open antagonism, they could not fail to observe my antipathy. I glory in the knowledge that I made conditions extremely uncomfortable for the more obnoxious of my masters. Crockery breaks very easily. Food sometimes gets cold, or can be insufficiently cooked, or indeed burned, time can pass unnoticed and meals brought late, and many other trivial yet irritating methods of reprisal are open, providing one does not indulge too freely in them and thus lay oneself open to the charge of studied insolence.

Soon the elderly captain declared that he had made arrangements to share a 'bunk', containing two beds, with his 'deah friend the Majah' who, on hearing of the distressing conditions under which the captain was having to exist, has so very kindly offered to share with him the luxury of a bunk which was serviced by a competent and obliging servant who knew his place. I had many passages with the R.N.A.S. officer, and at length I was called to the presence one morning and notified that arrangements had been made for me to be transferred to the next room—

No. 14. I said, 'Thanks very much, sir, will that be all?' I was told that I was the most inefficient batman it had ever been his misfortune to meet, to which I again said, 'Thank you very much, sir', just as politely.

Dykes was luckier with the next two groups of Crefeld officers he served as batman: eight Mercantile Marine officers ('not of the same standing, socially, as the lordly ones of Room 13, but to my prejudiced eye, far better men'), and six Australians, of whom he writes:

I was treated as one of them, and for the first time since coming to Crefeld I felt as if I belonged. These officers from the Antipodes were of a friendly disposition, and laughed and joked and made fun. I don't think they knew the meaning of dignity, at least they did not stand on it.

As often as was permitted Dykes was a spectator of the camp entertainments in which Lyall Grant took such an active part, though he was just as appreciative of the film shows ('Animated Pictures') and the Sunday orchestral concerts.

Plays and sketches were presented at frequent intervals by an enthusiastic and quite efficient caste of actors and 'actresses'. The orderlies were permitted to witness the presentations. One night there was a completely new departure. It was named 'Orderlies' Night', and on this occasion the tables were completely turned; officers supplied victuals, we had a good feed, being waited upon by the officers, who also were obliging enough to supply us with cigarettes, and a concert was given afterwards in our honour. The experience was a very pleasant one for us, but it didn't continue long enough for us to decide whether we really liked it, the following morning finding us back at our menial tasks of bedmaking, boots and button cleaning etc.

The soccer championship was the one occasion when officers and orderlies met on a truly equal footing, no holds barred, even though the better fed officers did have a slight physical advantage. The camp was divided into two rival factions, the 'regular' Crefeld officers and orderlies and the Gütersloh newcomers. After trouncing the Gütersloh and then the Crefeld teams of officers, a combined team of orderlies prepared to do battle with the combined might of their masters, and in Dykes' description one can sense the pent-up feelings that must have erupted among the more downtrodden of the orderly spectators as battle was joined.

As was only to be expected, these defeats rankled with the officers and put them on their mettle, and the following Sunday saw a strong combination of Crefeld and Gütersloh officers opposed to the triumphant orderlies, who nevertheless proceeded to demonstrate their superiority yet again by inflicting yet another whacking to the officers amidst the great jubilation of their supporters.

Then the officers went the whole hog and turned out the strongest side they could muster on the following Sunday. The camp turned out almost *en masse* for the epic struggle. A ding-dong battle ensued, both sides sparing no effort in the endeavour to win the day, but after a rattling good game neither goal had succumbed, and the respective defences had proved too strong for the opposing attacks, leaving the issue undecided. Of course it was unthinkable that the matter of superiority should be left undecided, and in deference to the generally expressed desire of officers and orderlies alike, the Officers' Sport Committee decided to postpone the scheduled commencement of the Tennis Season for a week.

Both officers' and orderlies' teams put in some practice during the following week (the orderlies when they could be spared a few minutes from their duties), and the afternoon of Sunday, 6 May discovered the teams lined up facing each other again, grimly determined to prevail, whilst an eager crowd looked on in anticipation of another titantic struggle.

This replay was also a great game, hard and cleanly fought, with no quarter asked or given, and both defences still prevailing, so that at the end of the period of play there was still no score, and it appeared that stalemate had been reached. The Sports Committee decided that it wasn't possible to extend the football season yet another week, and both teams being willing, nay anxious, to continue the struggle, it was decided to play extra time.

And so the combat continued, and still the defences held out heroically, until finally the orderlies, who didn't appear to have the stamina of the officers, faltered, and the officers' forward line succeeded in scoring the goal which had eluded them so long, thus triumphing in a match which reflected credit on both teams equally.

It is interesting to note how this 'titanic struggle' appeared to Lyall Grant. In a brief (and seemingly inaccurate) diary entry for 6 May he notes: 'Sunday, and the only event of interest was the last soccer match of the season—and I hope the last here. It was between officers and orderlies and as their match last Sunday was a draw there was much interest. The former won by 2–0.'

Two weeks later (with rumours rife among orderlies as well as officers that the hungry housewives of Crefeld were preparing to storm the camp stores) the British prisoners were on their way to Schwarmstedt. Dykes' comparison between the 'breaking-up parties' of the British officers and orderlies are illuminating. (As might be expected Lyall Grant makes no mention of any 'downstairs' festivities.)

The last evening of our stay at Crefeld was the occasion of another wild outburst on the part of the officers, and in a much minor degree of the orderlies. Pandemonium reigned, and the Germans did not appear to concern themselves with it at all. The night culminated in the building up and lighting of a huge bonfire on the square. The officers joined hands and danced round the fire, making the square re-echo with their shouts and cries, more after the manner of Red Indians than of civilized men.

Very many of them had 'soaked' themselves far more than was good for them, and some were dangerously drunk, but they were got away by their more sober and sensible friends and deposited where they couldn't do any harm. The revelry continued well on into the night, and I know there were many weary and fat heads the following day.

McDonald and I, who from our arrival in the camp had struck up a friendship with the French cooks, who appeared to be fixtures at Crefeld and were responsible for all the cooking, were invited to join them in a farewell feed, which we were proud to learn was being given in our honour. It took place in the cook-house. All the Frenchmen in the camp were present and we were the only Englishmen.

To say that the feed was sumptuous is to put it mildly. The dishes were many and varied, and all were exquisitely prepared and delightfully served. Both Mac and I were unashamedly full to repletion by the time the feast had run its course, or rather courses. It was with many protestations of lifelong friendship, and with many expressions of confidence in the invincibility of the *Entente Cordiale*, that we took leave of the Frenchmen well after midnight and staggered away in the direction of our quarters in the stables.

We found most of the orderlies still making merry, and expressing their firm intention of continuing to make merry until parade time, which had been set, as we thought, ridiculously early, making it necessary for we servants to be up and doing by 4 am. We knew the majority of officers would be quite incapable of getting their valises and other belongings ready for the evacuation!

Mac and I were in complete agreement that we should 'make a

night of it'. I rather fancy my zeal exceeded my powers, and I have no recollection of the next few hours. At least I hadn't to dress when it was time to be getting up, though I then experienced a complete revulsion of feeling, and thought how pleasant bed would be. Few if any of us felt in form for the strenuous day confronting us.

There are echoes of Lyall Grant 'nearly throwing a fit' at the sight of Schwarmstedt in Dykes' comment that 'the officers were very restless on arrival at the new camp'. He himself found it 'a lovely place for a Summer Camp, though not at all inviting in the winter'. For the first month he served without distinction as mess waiter at a table of eight officers in the dining-room. The 'last straw' was an occasion when he mistakenly put sugar in with the vegetables and potatoes instead of salt. He was exchanged for the assistant to the sanitary orderly, and spent his last three months at Schwarmstedt looking after the camp drains, devoting his spare time to improving the amenities for orderlies (including the construction of an elaborate putting green, with lengths of drainpipe for hazards).

But it is the restlessness of the officers that forms the main theme of this section of Dykes' journal. Escape, as Lyall Grant indicates, was very much in the air. What he does not indicate is the extent to which officers were assisted by orderlies in their escape bids. Here at least differences in rank or class could be forgotten in a common defiance of the enemy. This cooperation even went so far as officers masquerading as orderlies.

One method of escape which provided officers with the first step on the long journey to Holland was the substitution of officers for mess orderlies. The soup dixies had to be brought into the camp from the cookhouse which was outside the camp by twelve orderlies. Clever substitutions were practised, and a number of officers got away. There was also a fatigue party of orderlies required each day to collect waste paper, empty cans and other refuse, and dump it outside the camp, there to be collected by the Germans and taken off to provide material for the war effort. In these parties, too, officers dressed as orderlies got away.

It was Dykes' own implication in an escape plot that finally put an end to his nine months' masquerade as chambermaid, valet, waiter and char, and his banishment back to the cold comforts of the 'men's camps'. His role in the plot at least served as useful practice for the hatching of his own escape plot a year later.

Schwarmstedt Camp was built in the centre of a clearing, with dense woods a quarter to half a mile away. Much timber was wanted in the camp, a lot of it for the officers, who practised carpentry and the like. Each day, from two to six pm, a party of ten orderlies, accompanied by two guards, went to collect wood which had been felled in the morning.

This daily routine was observed by two officers, Major Fox and Naval Lieut Groves, and it occurred to them that here was an admirable opportunity of getting away from the confines of the camp. All they needed to do was to persuade two of the orderlies detailed for this work to allow them to take their places. The orderlies were to be given sufficient recompense for standing down and for the punishment which would inevitably follow the discovery of the escape and their part in it.

Arrangements had to be made for a suitable hiding place for the civilian clothing they would need once out of the camp, as well as the food they would require, map, compass, spare socks and other incidentals. If they looked in the least 'bulky' going out as orderlies with a working party, suspicions might be aroused.

One of the two officers approached me and, after explaining the scheme, asked if I knew a trustworthy French prisoner in the camp, who went out to work every day, who would be prepared to 'plant' sundry packages in a place where they would be well hidden but readily found by someone knowing where to look. I could suggest any recompense that I thought suitable.

There were a few French and Russian working parties in the camp, who would be above suspicion so far as an escape plot was concerned. I knew a number of the Frenchmen, whom I had cultivated for French language purposes, and readily undertook the commission. I had a man in mind, and when I approached him, he expressed his willingness to act.

For obvious reasons he was only able to take a little each day, and some time elapsed before everything was in readiness. He found a very suitable place as a cache, and drew a plan giving concise directions. I, of course, had had to be particularly careful that the Frenchman and I were not observed passing things through the partition wire that separated our two compounds, and we never met at the same time any day. Everything went according to plan. He was well paid for his cooperation, in cash and kind, and was highly delighted.

Careful, but unobtrusive, observations were kept on the sentry at the gate dividing officers' and orderlies' quarters, through which the two disguised officers would have to pass. It was observed that one particular guard was less vigilant than the others. The officers walked past him in borrowed orderly clothing without trouble, and we in the orderlies' quarters found ourselves acting host for a short time to two 'distinguished visitors', who were quite obviously keyed up for the occasion. They had rather foolishly overdone the resemblance to orderlies by deliberately besmudging their faces. If the guard had been observant he may have wondered why they had dirty faces, and made enquiries! I thought it was rather indiscreet, and remarked that 'the orderlies do wash sometimes, sir!' This drew an apology.

Major Fox succeeded in getting back to 'Blighty' via Holland. Lieut

Groves' feet gave out some twenty miles from the Dutch border and freedom. The two orderlies who had made their escape possible were given ten days' solitary confinement. Dykes' name went high up on a 'black list' of 32 orderlies (about half the full complement) suspected of assisting in officer escapes, not to be trusted again in the role of Private Jeeves. Dykes' experiences in other rank PoW camps for the rest of the war, his valiant but unsuccessful attempt to escape, his return to England as late as January, 1919, is another story. These extracts might suitably end with his brief account of his last night at Schwarmstedt on 7 September, 1917, an expression of end-of-the-term, lump-in-the-throat camaraderie that Lyall Grant would have appreciated.

The last night for the 'doomed' at Schwarstedt was spent in lively fashion, each man being determined to make the most of the time remaining to him in surroundings approaching affluence, or as nearly approaching that state as was possible for prisoners of war in Germany.

The officers *en bloc* had wished us the best of luck, and individually would have loaded us with any and every type of tinned goods, articles of clothing, books, or anything else either useful or merely ornamental which we might have desired, but which we could not possibly hope to take with us because of the insurmountable difficulties of transport.

Friendships which had been formed months before were in some cases to be dissolved, and many of these hard-bitten fellows showed, even though very faintly, that there was a trace of sentiment in their make-up. McDonald and I were still to be together, we had continued to form a partnership of two the whole time we had been with the officers, and had got along admirably together, so that the anxiety we felt regarding what lay before us was allayed by the knowledge that we should still be together.

It is revealing to compare the impact that prolonged confinement behind barbed wire had on the lives of Lyall Grant and Dykes, officer and orderly, extrovert and introvert. For Lyall Grant, his diary locked away, it was an episode to be forgotten, except in a detached way later in the jovial 'Old Boys' reunion' ambience of the Officer Prisoner of War (1914–18) Dining Club he used to attend. For Dykes, who has never since met one of his old PoW 'mucking-in chums', it is still an obsessive memory.

Repatriated in 1919 at the age of 21, Dykes found librarian posts occupied by women, and it was during six months on the dole that he wrote up his PoW experiences from the tiny notebooks he had kept secret from the Germans ('It all came back to me,' he recalls). Publishers were not interested. ('They said the market was flooded with ex-servicemen authors who thought they could write best-sellers.') He laid his 'masterpiece' aside.

Forty years later, during which Dykes' jobs had ranged from oil company salesman and depot manager to storekeeper and village sub-postmaster, his married daughter spotted the seven handwritten volumes in a bookcase.

'She was staying with us on holiday with her family, and, having nothing better to do one rainy day, dipped into them. She became absorbed. And it was because of her enthusiasm that I set to and laboriously typed out those thousands and thousands of words, using the "two-finger" method, condensing as I went along.

'I could fill a book with the details of the numerous attempts we have made since then to get it published. Visions of fame and notoriety faded away. Then I read that the Imperial War Museum was looking for war manuscripts and I sent it them. They wrote saying it was the most detailed and authentic account of its kind they had come across and that they would like to make a microfilm of it for their archives. Fame at last! My name would go down to posterity!'

At his home in Great Sutton, Cheshire, Dykes would appear to have all that could be wished for a contented old age: a loving wife, daughter and three grandchildren, reasonable health and mobility, a love of music and books, a caravan in the garage at the end of his kitchen garden. But he craves more than that niche in a museum's archives.

Like so many unsung non-heroes of the two world wars, he looks back at the most traumatic experiences of an otherwise conventional life and wonders what they were worth, if they had any meaning.

'Two of my brothers, now dead, made a name for themselves locally,' he says. 'One, a musician, with an opera group and orchestra. The other as landlord of a splendid country inn. Before I die I would dearly like to be recognized as having done something worthy of note.'

Chapter Six

DREAMING OF CREAM BUNS

SAPPER GEORGE WAYMARK

'We didn't know Jerry was there till we looked up from our dugouts and saw a long line of grey uniforms coming towards us in the dawn light. Our headquarters was quickly surrounded. There was no chance of putting up a fight. We were all taken—the Brigadier-General, the lot.'

Seated by the fireside in his home at Caterham, Surrey, George Waymark looks back 59 years to that early morning of 12 April, 1918, which for him began the eight most terrible months of his life. He was Sapper Waymark then, aged 24, a morse operator attached to a brigade headquarters of the 51st Division on the British Northern Front in Flanders. A habit he had acquired since arriving in France in June, 1915, had been the keeping of a diary. Secretively after his capture he continued to do so. It is a unique record of what it was like to be a prisoner behind the German lines during the closing stages of the war.

Three weeks before Waymark's capture, on 21 March, the Germans had launched the all-out offensive they confidently believed would win them the war. Flushed with success, they formed many of the prisoners they had captured as they overran the Allied lines into working parties behind their own lines. The early part of the diary gives a glimpse of what must have been the most macabre and frustrating of PoW experiences: that of being put to menial tasks under armed guard within sight of the British front line, the wrong side of no-man's-land.

Waymark's is the only diary among a number of harrowing accounts acquired by the Imperial War Museum from former PoWs captured during the 1918 German offensive. Though sporadic and tersely written, it has an immediacy and authenticity that no journal account written from memory can provide. That he managed to keep a diary at all was something of an achievement.

'I wrote the diary at night when we were locked in,' Waymark recalls. 'Fortunately we were only searched twice and on both occasions I was able to secrete my little notebook. I also managed to hold on to my watch by getting someone to tie it on to my braces at the back. It was the only watch in my camp. Not that time had much meaning for us. I was not always certain of the dates for the diary. And there are long gaps in it. You have to read monotony and exhaustion into them. Most of all you have to remember that for prisoners like us there was one constant obsession—FOOD.'

One of Waymark's most poignant diary entries records how every spare minute in working parties was spent talking about food, and how one fellow prisoner, a confectioner by trade, 'tells me glorious yarns of cream buns, eclairs etc'. Semi-starvation is the theme of all the similar accounts. Unlike those sent to PoW camps in Germany, these unfortunates were out of reach of the food parcels from home so essential to supplementing the meagre German ration of black bread and what passed for soup.

It was cold comfort to discover that German troops in rear areas were almost equally gnawed by hunger. Meat was non-existent. They had no equivalent to the Tommy's canteen. The Allied blockade, as much as the Allied armies, was bringing Germany to her knees. But of this Waymark was unaware as he began his eight months' purgatory, so near, yet so far, from the ebb and flow of battle.

12 April, 1918. Captured this morning at 5.0 am at Le Cornet Malo. Had no chance. Completely surrounded. Jerry relieved each one of their valuables, even taking the leather gaiters of a despatch rider. I had previously hung my watch on my braces at the back and got away with it. Carrying wounded until 7.0 pm. Wounded laid out in rows in paddock adjoining farm at Neuve Chapelle. Only one doctor and one Red Cross man to attend

them. Absolute chaos. Bandages made of paper. Had no food since last night.

13 April. Slept in open last night. There was a frost. Had some boiled potatoes this morning. First food we have had. Went round rows of wounded and picked out the dead for burial. Dug a hole about 9′ wide, 14′ long and 6′ deep. Into this we had to place dead bodies, head towards the outer edge. Four or five rows like this, and we had to stand on dead to lay them in evenly. One of the last was an old French lady who had been 'killed' the day before. Before she was placed with the remainder, I distinctly saw her hand move. I pointed this out to Jerry by saying '*nix mort*' but the only reply was '*Yaa*'. I insisted that the old lady was alive, but Jerry stopped further argument with an application of his boot. I am certain that she was buried alive.

The last body to be placed in the hole was that of one of our airmen, whose machine was brought down the day before about 100 yards away. He was terribly injured about the head, but I knew by the absence of blood that he was dead before the machine crashed. I had to search his pockets for anything that would identify him, but there was nothing. His shoulder straps had South Africa on them and one of these I cut off and gave to Jerry. When the earth was filled in, the top body was only about a foot below ground level. No burial service, nothing to mark who or what they were, English, German and a civilian all together, poor devils.

14 April. After complaining about food or the lack of it, we were given a wounded man between four and told to follow the road. We didn't know where we were going, but wherever it was it couldn't be worse than Neuve Chapelle. On the way our shells fell quite close enough and I'm afraid the wounded had a rough passage. It was natural to duck when shells were about and as we didn't all duck together, the stretcher wasn't always level. We left the wounded at a house after walking about four hours and

made our way to Marquilles, where there was a prison camp. Hungry as can be. Only boiled potatoes since we were taken prisoners. We were looking forward to a meal when we arrived at this camp but we were disappointed. Eight men to a small loaf in the morning and at 6 p.m.

15 April. Commenced work this morning at 7.0 am. Thank goodness that night is over. Accommodation awful. Sleeping in a hut. Beds limited. Scores slept on the floor which is in a filthy condition. A relief to get out into the fresh air. Work consists of carrying bricks. On eight to a loaf too.

17 April. Still here. Hoping each day to leave for a proper camp. One of the guard gave me a herring today. Never tasted raw fish before, but then I have never been so hungry. Guard told me (in broken French) that fish was exported from England to Holland who sold it to feed the German troops. If such is the case, what a farce.

21 April. Went for a bath this morning and had clothes fumigated. Mine wanted it badly. Shirt almost walking, although I have tried to keep the little devils down. Taken to a camp at Illies afterwards. Food is supposed to be better here. I hope so. I'm feeling as weak as can be. This place looks as though it might have been a brewery but the inside has been taken out. Beds, consisting of stout wire netting are in four rows along the wall. Each bed about 3′ wide and about 4′ between each row. My bed is at the top and I have to climb 16′ to reach it. Two of us occupy each bed. Wire netting has stretched—result, we both have to sleep facing the same way. When one gets tired on that side he wakes the other one up and suggests turning over. Amusing under different circumstances.

22 April. Paraded at 5.0 am. Interpreter asked if anyone wanted to go sick and one man unwisely said he did. The officer came and looked at him, and then gave him a punch in the face which knocked him down. He had to march with the rest of us.

We were taken to Frohmelles where we had to repair roads. Jerry had pushed forward at this point and we were working inside a horseshoe. No-man's-land was here somewhere, and the place is a shambles.

30 April. We are still at this awful place. The walk to Frohmelles and back each day is getting me down. Yesterday we saw one of our men tied to a tree when we got back and found that he had stolen a piece of bread belonging to one of the men. Our men had therefore tied him up as a punishment. I don't know how long he had been there, but I can imagine the feeling which prompted him to steal the bread, gnawing hunger.

2 May. Still going to Frohmelles each day. Hungrier, if that is possible. Food absolutely awful. Talking to German guard. He came from Alsace and spoke French. He was about 60 years old and quite a decent sort. He was tired of the war. He had a son who was a prisoner in the Isle of Man. Before he was taken prisoner he was rather thin, but a photo taken since he was in the Isle of Man showed that he was now quite fat. And we are starving. He said he wished the English would attempt to close the horseshoe and take him prisoner. He didn't wish it any more than I did. On our way back each day we can see our front line and at night the star shells only look about a mile away. How I should like to get back there. I'm seriously thinking of trying.

1 June. Absolutely fed up. We have an idea that Jerry is selling our rations to outside Germans, but what can we do? My boots are beginning to go home. Don't know what will happen when they are gone. Found a tin of Fray Bentos in one of the trenches today. First meat I've tasted since I have been a prisoner. I never realized until now how good bully beef is. Talking with Tilburn, a metropolitan policeman, today. He is willing to try and reach those star shells with me.

3 June. Escaped last night about 11.30 pm. My pliers had not been taken away and I was able to cut through the barbed wire

when the sentry was at the other end of his beat. It took about half an hour. On our way, climbed over several reserve trenches, couldn't help thinking what works of art they are. Far better than ours. We made good progress until about 3.0 am and then we ran into a German sentry. He shouted something but we didn't stop to argue and in our flight ran into a line of barbed wire. We got through it, but I left part of my coat in the middle of it. After this we thought it best to wait until it was dark again, so found a large shell hole to sleep in. By this time it was nearly light and we could see German transport passing along a road about fifty yards away. We were not spotted, however.

4 June. Had to wait until 11.30 last night because the moon was up. When we did start the excitement started too. Hiding about every 10 minutes, challenged 4 or 5 times, fired at from about 10 or 12 yards. 3 times. What a hell of a lot of sentries they have got. Once we dropped down into a ditch over which was a plank which was used as a bridge. I was immediately underneath it and just then a working party carrying stores etc up to the line, passed over it. I could have touched them with my hand.

Getting very near those star shells and our own machine guns seem to be busy because we had to fall down two or three times to prevent being hit by them. About 3.0 am we were nearly there but as it was getting light we should have waited another day, but we risked crossing the last trench and were caught. Tilburn had gone first but he suddenly rolled back on to my arms, which were extended, and left my head exposed above his back. I was in that position when Jerry put his rifle to my head and said 'Loose'. (This seems to be a word generally in use by the Germans and indicates anything from 'put 'em up' to 'get a move on'.)

Taken back to Annoeullin, passing through La Bassée on the way. We passed numbers of Germans, one of whom was very encouraging. He pointed his finger to his forehead and said:

'Morgin come, capoot, eh?', meaning we should be shot in the morning. At Annoeullin we saw an officer, a splendid specimen of a man, over 6′ tall. Wore a monocle. Spoke English. Had long talk with him. He could not understand why we wanted to get back to our lines. He said we had plenty of everything and were safe, but when I told him that the Germans were existing chiefly on potatoes and that our soldiers had plenty of everything he seemed surprised and hardly believed white bread was issued as well as fresh meat. Taken back to Illies by cavalry man. Placed in guard room on bread and water.

6 June. Released from guard room tonight. Nice to stretch one's legs after a cell measuring about 5′ by 8′.

7 June. Tilburn and me evidently regarded as dangerous because we were not sent to Frohmelles with the others. Instead we had to do odd jobs in and near the camp and wherever we went an armed guard was with us. Had quite an easy day and the guard was a decent sort. Had a bath today, first since we have been here. Needless to say, I wanted it. Absolutely lousy. Can't keep the blighters under and we have no water to wash in. I've cut my nails down as far as possible to prevent myself scratching and so causing septic sores. One or two places on my legs don't look at all healthy.

10 June. Thank goodness we have left Illies. Started from there at 8.0 this morning and arrived at Carvin about noon. Didn't get any food until 3.0. We think we are waiting here for a train to take us to a proper prisoners' camp in Germany. Sleeping in a two-storey building which is filthier than Illies, if that is possible. No work to do, just lazing about.

12 June. Haven't moved yet. Food awful. Boiled cabbage and bread. There is another camp quite close and we have to march there for our dinner. Yesterday our planes bombed Carvin and two bombs fell in this camp, killing three of our men. What atrocious luck, after getting through Jerry's bombardment on

23 March. Heard a man sing *Mother Macree* today and its effect on everyone was remarkable. Although there were about 200 men on this floor and there was a terrific din, yet he didn't sing more than a few words before there was a dead silence, which remained until he had finished. I had a talk with him afterwards and he told me he was in York Minster choir. I can well believe it, he had a glorious voice.

14 June. Tilburn and I paraded at 6 o'clock this morning and started away about 8 o'clock under a guard. Arrived at Lille about midday and left later by train. About 4 o'clock arrived at St Amand and then started to march again. It's now about 5.30 pm and we are resting by the roadside.

22 June. Haven't been able to make an entry since the 14th. About 7 pm that day we arrived at Fort Flinnes. This is close to the Belgian frontier and was apparently built by the French to protect their frontier. Mortagne is only about a mile away. It consists of a huge mound surrounded by a moat and all the offices are built on the French side of it. The cells run a long way under the mound and are in complete darkness.

When we arrived on the 14th we were searched, given a piece of bread and some water and placed in these cells. Once a day Jerry came and brought us our ration of bread and water and then we were left until the following day. My cell was about 5′ by 8′. I couldn't see how high it was. A board was supplied for a bed and as I lay there I could feel the insects running over me in droves. Perhaps it is just as well I could not see in what a condition it was. Each night I went through the Church service, being Parson, Choir and Congregation, and, strange to say, some of the others in nearby cells joined in the hymns.

We were let out this afternoon and I was truly glad to see daylight. We are a mixed lot—British, Portuguese, Italians, French and Russians. The latter do not sleep in the same room as the remainder. They have one to themselves. The Russkies are a poor specimen of men; if the others are no better, then I'm not surprised they couldn't fight. The Froggies seem to be better off than the others – they are receiving parcels of biscuits etc, in addition to the food Jerry gives us. We are told (Tilburn and me) that we have three months' imprisonment to serve for breaking away from the camp at Illies. I suppose they have a standard of punishment, because there was no trial.

27 June. Been here nearly two weeks and dislike it more every day. We are fetched out at 5.0 am and one swine (a Prussian) delights in using his bayonet for this purpose. Sawing wood until 6.30 am when we are given a kind of tea. At 7.0 am we start for the Fabric which is on the other side of Mortagne. We pass over the River Scheldt and a Canal to get to it. I don't know why the place is called the Fabric. It was evidently a large workshop of some sort, but all the machines had been removed. Our job has been to shift sand from the barges to the railway trucks. One man throws it from the barge to another man who throws it about three yards to the next man, and so on until it reaches the trucks. The treadmill would be a pastime to it.

One of the guards (another Prussian) has an Alsatian dog which he sets at those he thinks are not working fast enough. I've seen a number of men suddenly bowled over by the dog with it standing over them with bared teeth at their throat. Beyond a scratch I don't think the dog bit them, but the effect on the men so treated can be imagined. The Prussian thought it a huge joke and would double up with laughter before he called the dog off. We go back to the Fort at 1 o'clock for soup (boiled cabbage) and return to the Fabric about 2 o'clock. We finish at 5.30 pm, when we get a piece of bread and more tea (?). At 6.30 pm we are locked up for the night.

30 June. This afternoon we were supposed to wash our shirts. Two tubs of water were given us and in these 100 shirts had to be washed. We have only one shirt each and as there was no means

of drying them, I'm afraid that many of them were put on wet after washing. I managed to wet only the sleeves of mine without the guard noticing that the remainder of it was dry. How could 50 men wash filthy shirts in a tub of cold water without soap? Everyone was ordered to have his hair cut close with clippers and Jerry would of course choose to shout 'fall in' (in German) when only half of mine was cut. Our beds, which are made of plaited straw, are alive with lice, and I have slept on a form about eight inches wide for some nights now.

1 July. Moving more sand today, but in a different place. We had to load sand into trucks from the ground, about six of us to each truck. I had to throw in at the end over the top which was about 9′ high. Done to the wide when we had finished. I'm wondering how much longer I can last.

3 July. Jerry apparently has all the sand he wants, because we have been unloading wood from trucks today. This is the worst job yet. Stripped to the waist, blinded with perspiration and swines of guards, I couldn't stand up when we had finished. How long will this last?

7 July. Saw a Jerry hit an Italian with the butt of his rifle this morning and he has an eye like a prize-fighter. On our way back to the fort our planes bombed the town and we had to run. The civvies had a communion or something on, because all the girls were going to church dressed in white. One bomb fell just outside the church but fortunately no one was hit. Taken to the river this afternoon for a bathe. The mud at the bottom was over our knees so the only thing to do was swim about. Some couldn't swim and they clung to the bank to prevent themselves sinking in the mud. Before we had been there five minutes, the swine with the Alsatian came along and set the dog at those who were holding on to the bank.

9 July. A Rumanian arrived this morning. When I asked him what he was, he said 'Roman'. If I'd known what it was in French

I might have asked him where his armour and spear was. Still carrying wood.

10 July. More excitement today. There was another raid over the town; we lay in the grass just outside and had a good view of the planes flying in formation. The Rumanian didn't stay long; he escaped this morning. Don't know how he did it. Damned smart. We were immediately marched back to the fort, formed up in fours, marched up and down the yard, turning heads left or right each time we passed the officer in charge. He was standing at the side shouting at the top of his voice and firing his revolver over our heads when we passed him. He seemed to be blaming us for the Rumanian's escape, the *swiner Englander*.

12 July. Two of the Froggies left today. I think they are going back to their camp. Before they went one of them offered me some biscuits for my riding bags, and after some arguing I accepted 20 biscuits and an old pair of cord trousers. Whatever would they say at home if they were to see me now. I never thought that I should sell my clothes for food, but I have reached the stage when the one and only thought is food.

Every time we have a spare minute we are talking of what food we used to have before the war and what we would have when we got back. There is one man here who is a confectioner, lives at Easton near Winchester or Chichester. He and I are about the same height and we therefore get together for wood carrying. He tells me glorious yarns of cream buns, eclairs, etc. Yesterday on our way down to the Fabric we saw some raw potato peelings on the side of the road and there was a blind dash and a fight to get them. The guards wondered what was the matter, I think, but they soon set about us with the butts of their rifles. There were no peelings left when we got up.

As we were lined up for our cabbage soup today, the swine with the Alsatian came out of the cook-house with a large dish of dinner totally different to that which we get. He offered it to the leading man, who went to take it with both hands, but he was pushed back and the dinner was placed on the ground for the dog and we had to stand there and watch. I should have regarded that dinner as a banquet.

13 July. We are all suffering more or less with swelling in some part of the body. One or two men have faces so large that their eyes are hardly visible. It affects me in the legs and I can only think it is due to the watery food we are getting. Today I have been put in the sick bay with instructions to keep my feet up.

22 July. Been in the sick bay since last entry. Swelling gone and legs as thin as sticks.

26 July. Returned to work this morning and started on the eternal wood carrying.

28 July. Allowed to send a postcard home today. The first since I was taken prisoner. I'm afraid it contained nothing but request for food. Have no boots now so am wearing sabots. Working just outside the fort. These guards are better and one of them today gave me a drink of what he called schnapps. It was good too, put new life in me. We are making trenches for the infantry to practise in.

18 August. Legs have swollen again but I've had to work. One day I walked down in some German infantry boots which Jerry had given me, but they hurt so much I had to take them off. When I tried to put them on again, I found that the swelling was so bad that I couldn't get them on again, so I had to walk back without boots.

12 September. Been in sick bay again with legs, but swelling has gone down again. Been raining hard for three days and we are walking through water over our boot tops when wood carrying. No means of drying anything when we get back, with the result that we sleep in wet clothes and start the next day in the same way.

15 September. Got a fresh job. Digging potatoes and carrying them to the fort. No need to eat peelings now. Saw infantry

training with machine guns in trenches we had made. Wonderful work. Their marching is a picture to watch and harmonized singing seems to be part of their training. One of the guards is a decent sort. Today he said to me, 'Tommy, langsam, Officier come loose, eh?', meaning we could take it easy but if an officer came along to get a move on.

When carrying the potatoes into the fort store, I saw a packet on a table and thinking it might be food, I took it. It was honey and jolly good too. About an hour afterwards everyone was paraded in the yard and the billets searched by Jerry. Bushels of potatoes which had been taken in by the prisoners were found, but no trace of the honey which, by the way, belonged to the officer. One of our men gave me away and I was given five days cells.

1 October. This place is hell. Englanders can't do anything right. No bath for months and we are walking with lice. Impossible to get rid of them. Think and talk of nothing but food.

6 October. It's getting cold now. Should like some more clothes to wear. There is excitement in the air because our boys are rumoured to be advancing.

8 October. Great excitement. Saw a line of observation balloons on our way back from the Fabric today. They were a long way away, but we haven't seen them before.

9 October. Balloons are nearer today and shrapnel was bursting near them. Civvies are excited.

12 October. Balloons still nearer today and behind them another line. We know that our boys are advancing fast and that the second line of balloons are our own.

14 October. Jerry preparing to leave. All civvies are being sent back and Jerry is blowing up houses, dumps and bridges. It's rather sad to see the civvies leaving with as many of their belongings as possible, but they all speak very hopefully. Had some

baked potatoes today and they were lovely. Threaded about 12 on a piece of wire and pushed them down the chimney of the copper, which stands in the yard and which is used to boil our water. I got them back when we came back from the Fabric and Jerry wasn't looking. They were rather black but they were good.

15 October. We left the Fort about midday today and walked to Collonelle, where we entrained about 7.0 pm. Wonder where we are going now.

17 October. Still in the train with scarcely any food. One of the men had a tin and we were able to boil some potatoes, which we had brought with us. We made a fire in the compartment and used the wood from the luggage racks for the purpose. Held coats over the windows so that Jerry should not see the fire. Nearly choked, but we had something to eat. The wonder is that the compartment didn't catch fire.

18 October. Still don't know where we are going. At one station where we stopped, a German girl about 8 or 9 years old came to the window and said, '*Brood*'. She was apparently asking us for bread and it struck me as being as good a mixture of humour and tragedy as one could get. Humorous, because we would have given anything for a piece of bread, and tragic, because the youngster, who was quite respectably dressed, should be reduced to asking prisoners of war for bread. Unfortunately one of the guards heard her and he gave her a smack on the side of the face which sent her tumbling into some Germans who were standing near. I couldn't help wondering whether that youngster's father was fighting or whether he had gone the way of thousands more and been disposed of like those in the hole at Neuve Chapelle. Following the Rhine from Coblenz to Mainz and have never seen such scenery. If only we could be enjoying it under normal conditions.

19 October. Arrived at Worms about 8.0 pm and taken to

prison camp. Haven't lain down since we left the Fort and feel as though I should break in two pieces.

20 October. What a night! When we arrived last night we were given some soup and then went to sleep. About 10.30 pm there was a devil of a noise and about eight Jerries came and fetched everyone out of their bunk. We were counted, the room was inspected and then we were allowed to go back to sleep again. About 12.30 am the same thing happened again and at 2.30 am and 4.30 am it was repeated. I found out afterwards that some Froggies had previously occupied this room and during the night they tunnelled under the yard and on until they were out of the prison. About 40 of them escaped in this way and so the nightly visits were made to prevent a repetition. There are only English and French here, but there are hundreds of Ruskies in the compound adjoining. This camp seems to be much cleaner, so perhaps we shall have some peace from the everlasting lice. The food is awful. Two water soups and 12 to a loaf a day. The only consolation is that we have no work to do.

10 November. Glorious news today [*sic*]. Armistice signed and we expect to leave shortly. What a difference in the attitude of the guards towards the officer. Yesterday they would spring to attention when the officer was a mile off, but today they treat him as though he wasn't there. Their attitude towards us is different too. They don't seem to mind what we do. For example, we broke down the 10′ partition dividing us from the next camp and Jerry walked to the other end of the camp so that he should not see.

When we got in the other camp I saw two men, or rather skeletons, because they were nothing more. They wore khaki clothes and looked ghastly. I asked them who they were and what regiment they belonged to, but they had lost all power of speech. I don't know whether they were British or not, but they must have been treated hellishly to be in that condition. The Jerry NCO who delighted in making us stand with our faces to the wall, while he flourished his revolver and held forth about *swiner Englanders* and spat on the ground to show his hatred of us, has disappeared. Perhaps it's as well, because I feel sure some of the men now would give him a rough time.

Ten days later Waymark and his fellow-prisoners were sailing down the Rhine towards freedom. They reached Rotterdam on 26 November and were quartered in a warehouse on the quayside.

Lots of food here, but one's inside is so weak that ordinary food is too rich. At least that's how it affected me and I only had two sardines. YMCA giving away cigarettes. First I have smoked since being taken prisoner. Drew new clothes today.

27 November. Went on board at 10.0 am. I had on many occasions prayed for the big ship and here it was at last. Sailed about 4.0 pm. How good white bread tastes. To appreciate it, one must live on cabbage soup and German bread for eight months. I think it had been cooked on board and I made my first meal on board off that alone.

29 November. Tonight we arrived at Ripon. The boat docked at Hull about 2.30 pm and the noise made by the ships' sirens was deafening and it was pathetic to hear mothers and sisters asking whether John Smith or Tom Brown was on board. I wondered whether they would ever see those they were asking for, and whether either of those skeletons of men I saw at Worms would answer to either of those names. Owing to the kindness of a civilian whom I spoke to at the barrier when we disembarked, I was able to send a telegram home, notifying my arrival. He kindly defrayed the expense of the telegram, because I hadn't a penny.

1 December. Treated royally since we arrived here. Eggs and bacon and porridge for breakfast and as much of it as we want. We can all do with it, though. I weighed myself today and turned

the scale at 8 stone; before I was taken prisoner I weighed 12 stone 6 pounds. Given 3 months convalescent leave and left at 4.0 pm for London.

Now I can rest and try to imagine what I should do if I met some of those guards whose one aim in life seemed to be to make our existence a hell. I wonder!

Thousands of released prisoners of war were now flooding home from the war to end all wars. Some, like Farrant and Surrey Dane, captive for four years, had survived a greater ordeal than Waymark's. Some, like Lyall Grant, had suffered little more than the boredom and ignominy of encagement. Few, it would seem, harboured any lingering hatred for the Hun.

Today, a picture of octogenarian well-being, Waymark makes it clear that the 'swine' he harps on in his diary were the exception rather than the rule. 'It was the Prussian types we couldn't stand,' he says. 'Most were quite decent sorts, though hunger brought out the worst in all of us. Before being captured I had served on occasions in front line observation posts and never heard the Tommy talking about the Hun or the Boche. It was always Jerry, there was more fellow-feeling than hatred. All that stuff about "the only good German is a dead one" was Home Front propaganda.'

A Post Office clerk before enlisting, ex-Sapper Waymark took up his career where he had left off. In 1922 he married the girl he had dreamed of whilst a prisoner of war (when visions of cream buns and eclairs did not intrude). He rose to be Postmaster at Stony Stratford, Bucks, transferring to Caterham as Postmaster in 1944. During the Second World War he served with the Observer Corps ('using my morse in connection with MI5—but I mustn't say anything about that').

After the death of his first wife in 1943, he married again, a widow, and today his family circle includes five grandchildren and one great-grandchild. A trifle deaf, but still active, he looks back on a life of solid achievement, in which those days when he could write in a diary, 'This place is hell', and 'I'm wondering how much longer I can last', seem out of focus, in another dimension.

'When I re-read that diary it all comes back,' he says. 'But it was an experience worth going through. It has taught me to count my blessings.'

Chapter Seven

DEATH MARCH FROM KUT

RQMS FRANK HARVEY

ON 6 MAY, 1916, under the whips and rifle butts of their mounted Kurdish guards, 2,592 British soldiers, already emaciated after being five months under siege by the Turks, started off on a 1,200-mile forced march into a captivity which for all but 837 of them would end in death. Death from starvation and thirst, death from exposure to the blistering desert sun, death from exhaustion and disease, death from the knife-slashes of scavenging Arabs.

It happened during the campaign in Mesopotamia, one of the little publicised 'side-shows' of the First World War. The public outcry that followed the humiliating capitulation of the British garrison at Kut-al-Amara soon blew over. The death march itself was officially hushed up during the war, and even today there are few who have heard of it. Yet from hindsight it can be seen as signalling the beginning of the end for the British Empire.

The siege was the outcome of a rash attempt to capture Baghdad by a division of an expeditionary force of the Indian Army sent to Mesopotamia to protect the Royal Navy's oil supply in the Persian Gulf. After the bloody battle of Ctesiphon, 15 miles from Baghdad, some 10,000 British and Indian fighting men, 3,500 Indian non-combatants and 2,000 sick and wounded, withdrew to the fortress town of Kut on the banks of the Tigris. The siege lasted 147 days (the longest in our history). And, following hard on the catastrophic campaign in Gallipoli, the spectacle of a beleaguered British garrison being brought to its knees as supplies ran out and all attempts at relief were foiled was God's gift to the enemy propagandists.

God was, indeed, invoked (as an anti-British deity), in an impassioned attempt to inspire mutiny among the 6,000 Indian troops in

Kut. Bundles of pamphlets laid against the front line barbed wire called on the Indians to murder their British officers and desert to the Sultan. Purporting to have been written by Indians who had emigrated to America and who were now fighting for Germany and her allies, the pamphlet began: 'Oh Dear Indian Brethren. You understand the fact well that God has created this war for setting India free from the hands of the cruel English . . .' Most of the pamphlets were collected by the British. What few got through to the Indians did lead to a number of desertions. But on that death march into a brutal captivity there were still over three times as many Indians as British (some 9,300 including non-combatants).

As an undermining of the myth of an all-powerful, all-conquering British Raj, the capitulation at Kut was played for all it was worth. A British offer of two million pounds in gold in exchange for the repatriation of the captured garrison was summarily turned down by the Turks. Of far greater value in the long run would be the public flaunting of a master race brought low.

And so, across desert and mountain, to the crack of those bull-penis whips and cries of '*Yellah, yellah;*', stumbled the pathetic columns of skeletal scarecrows in khaki. In the flag-bedecked streets and bazaars of Baghdad and other Turkish towns they were spat upon, stoned, reviled. For the people of the Middle East and Far East it was a revelation: the British, too, could be humbled, degraded, enslaved.

At the head of one straggling column on this Via Dolorosa, a column largely comprising 252 men of the 2nd Battalion, the Dorsetshire Regiment, marched Regimental Quartermaster Sergeant Frank Harvey, aged 30, short (5 foot 4 inches) and stocky, every inch the tough, disciplined, dedicated Regular. He had enlisted at the age of 18 and was unmarried. The Army was his life, and in this supreme test of leadership, fortitude and stamina he did not fail.

Every day of the fifty agonising days it took to reach the working camps in Turkey, Harvey jotted diary entries in his field service notebook, later expanded into a narrative. It is a soldier's factual account, rarely betraying emotion, meticulously recording the starvation rations, the precise time of setting out on the next leg (sometimes as much as 30 miles in a day) and of arrival, half-dead from exhaustion, at the next bivouac, the constant clubbings, floggings and other brutalities perpetrated by the Kurdish cavalry escort under their sadistic commander, Lieutenant Mahomed Russi.

Harvey takes for granted his own role as senior NCO in charge of the column. He does not gloss over the occasion when he himself succumbed to exhaustion and dropped out of the column. But that his role was a crucial one in keeping up morale is apparent from the testimony of the last living survivor of that column (to be quoted later). What one must read between the lines is the example he set and the unflagging encouragement he gave to his men: 'Come on, boys, come on, come on, keep up . . .'

Tragically Harvey was killed in an insignificant affray in India three years after the end of the war. He had risen to the rank of Quartermaster Lieutenant, and it is thanks to a fellow officer that his diary-narrative was preserved. He had it privately printed in 1922 under the title *The Sufferings Of The Kut Garrison During Their March Into Turkey As Prisoners Of War*. In an introduction he wrote: 'Those who knew Harvey well will never forget him, a man with a very strong personality, and who at all times did all he could for others. Perhaps his greatest value was the wonderful power he had of distilling into all he met a PRIDE AND LOVE FOR THE REGIMENT which could not be surpassed . . .'

Harvey *was* forgotten and his diary-narrative was hailed as a notable discovery at the Imperial War Museum when a copy of the privately printed booklet was presented by Major-General H. H. Rich, who was a young infantry officer at Kut and who organized an annual reunion of survivors until his death in 1976. The narrative runs to over 45,000 words, and, for purposes of compression, much of the repetitive detail (particularly relating to the miniscule rations provided) have been omitted from the extracts that follow.

Harvey's diary account starts on the day of the surrender, 29 April, 1916, when the garrison was at least making sure that the Turkish victors found no spoils of war, apart from themselves. Stores were burned, ammunition thrown far out into the river to rust as quickly as possible, rifles broken up, high explosive charges rammed into the muzzles of guns and exploded.

Most of the troops were by now more suitable cases for nospital treatment than for a 1,200-mile forced march. 'For a considerable time we had been reduced to four ounces of bread and half pound of mule flesh, so the majority of our men were in a very bad state of health, and all were frightfully weak,' writes Harvey.

A final communique from their commander, Major-General Charles Townshend, stating that the Turkish Commander-in-Chief had shown himself 'full of admiration for our heroic defence of five months', held out hopes that he would soon be announcing the garrison's despatch for India, on condition that they did not serve again against the Turks. Townshend, who made reference to his own 'bodily illness and anguish of mind', ended with an exhortation: 'Whatever has happened, my comrades, you can only be proud of yourselves. We have done our duty. I ask you to stand by me with your ready and splendid discipline shown throughout . . .' Townshend was to spend the rest of the war in semi-luxury in Constantinople as an 'honoured guest' (his words) of the Turks, making no attempt to mediate on behalf of his suffering men.

On 30 April the captured garrison was marched to a Turkish camp at Shamran six miles north of Kut. The officers (220 British and 200 Indian) remained with their men until 4 May, when they were transported by paddle-steamer to Baghdad and marched, without coercion, 600 miles to the camps where they were to spend a relatively comfortable captivity. For the other ranks it was different.

It was on 6 May when I consider that our real troubles began. The order came that we were to get out for the march at once, this meant packing up all we could carry on our backs, and get a move on. I carried one blanket, one British warm coat, three pairs of socks, one extra shirt, auto strop safety razor, shaving brush, tooth brush, several tablets of soap, a field service note book (my diary), and a lot of other small items. In addition to this we had been advised to carry as much food as possible, so that with kit and rations we were well laden.

Just prior to moving camp we had been divided into groups or divisions. The one we were with was composed of the 2nd Battalion, The Dorsetshire Regiment, Details Indian Cavalry, 66th Punjabis and 104th Rifles. Our permanent escort had taken over the command of the column just as we were clear of the camp. They consisted of a regiment of Kurdish Cavalry. A squadron was told off as our escort under the command of Lieutenant Mahomed Russi.

Before we had been very long on the march we found our loads of kit and food a great burden, many men fell out through fatigue and were beaten along by the escort. Mahomed Russi rode up and down the column slashing with his whip at men every few yards. One of the Royal Navy contingent, marching a good distance ahead of the column I was in, fell out thoroughly exhausted, and by some means had been placed on a camel which was marching along a flank. When we were abreast of the camel, the sailor, who had apparently fainted through the effects of the heat, fell off the camel's back, but as he was tied to the camel, was being dragged along the ground almost under the camel's feet.

Several men of my regiment rushed out of the ranks to the assistance of the sailor, when Mahomed Russi and several of the escort galloped up and commenced to lash with whips and hit with the butts of their rifles any men who were out of the ranks. Meanwhile the sailor was being dragged along the ground and no attempt was made on the part of the escort to assist him; he was brought in dead that night.

We halted between six and seven o'clock that night thoroughly exhausted with fatigue. Our bivouac was along a canal, flowing out of the Tigris about a mile away. Our drinking water was out of this canal, but as we found throughout our marches, the Turkish Authorities made no provision to boil or chlorinate water to prevent disease. Right on the top of our drinking water supply were our latrines, and within five yards of where we slept.

The following morning, Sunday, 7 May, we were rudely awakened by our escort galloping madly through the camp about four o'clock and shouting, '*Yellah! Yellah!*' (This is an Arabic word meaning 'go on', or thereabouts.) The leading troops suffered mostly, as the escort, as soon as they reached their sleeping place, commenced to strike out right and left to get them on the march.

That day we marched from 0400 to 1500 hours and it was quite sufficient to break the hearts of much stronger men (physically) than we were. Many of our men were without water bottles and the sun being very powerful caused our thirst to be very acute, yet if we came near the river, our escort stood guard over it with their rifles and any one attempting to get a drink was beaten away.

Men who fell out that day from exhaustion, on their arrival at the halting place had some pitiful tales to relate of how they had been driven along and flogged. No rations were issued to us that day, either before starting or at the finish of the march.

On the morning of 8 May, we fully expected to have a repetition of the previous morning, and were packed up and ready to go soon after four o'clock, but nothing happened so we lay down again for a few hours. By 0700 hours the sun became too hot for us to lie about so we began to move about. Nothing particular happened during the day except a so-called Medical Inspection, at which some of our men who were particularly bad were told they would have to march to Baghdad unless they wanted to be left to die in the desert.

About 1800 hours we were ordered to draw rations and were marched to the Commandant's tent on the outskirts of the camp. Here were a few pack camels loaded with bags. They were unloaded and emptied on the ground, when we saw that their contents were chupatties, which were steaming from the perspiration of the camels, and reeked abominably. After being paraded first in one spot, then another, and then counted a few times, our portions were doled out to us, and when issued to the men they received a piece about the size of the palm of one's hand, very thin and mouldy. This was our first issue of rations since leaving Shamran Camp on the 6th.

Tuesday, 9 May was very much the same as on the previous day, but for rations we received three biscuits, which were black, very hard and composed of a mixture of barley meal, husks, straw and dirt . . .

On Wednesday, 10 May we commenced to march at 0530 hours and continued marching until 1200 hours, when we were halted by the Tigris. Rations were issued in the evening, when we received four of the usual black biscuits per man. By this time we had found the best way to eat these was to pound them as small as possible with the heel of the boot, soak them for a couple of hours, and then boil them for a time. It was impossible to eat them in their dry state, in fact it was impossible to break them except with a stone or the heel of a boot.

Thursday, 11 May. We again marched at 0500 hours and continued till about 1500 hours. This was a very hot and tiring march and numerous cases of flogging occurred through men being exhausted and falling out; no effort was made to provide any conveyance for those who were sick, several of whom fell out and were never seen again. Marches of this kind were terrible for those without water bottles, as the escort would not allow anyone near water when we passed it, flogging anyone who attempted to get near it.

No rations of any kind were issued this day, so we lay hungry on the desert for the night.

We continued our march at 0500 hours on Friday, 12 May, and halted at Azziyah at 1030 hours. During this march we passed Umm-al-Tabul, where the Turkish Forces overtook the 6th

Division on 1 December, 1915, during the retirement to Kut. All that could be seen on the ground were the bones of the casualties we had inflicted. For rations we received two of the usual biscuits.

On Saturday, 13 May, we marched from Azziyah at 0500 hours and halted at Zeur at 1330 hours. This was another hard march with plenty of floggings. During this march a sergeant of the Royal Flying Corps could not keep up with his Unit and was struggling along on the flank of the column, and when we came to where he was dragging himself along, several of the escort began to flog him unmercifully. Some of the men who saw this rushed out from the ranks and dragged the sergeant into our ranks to protect him, but about a dozen of the escort galloped into their midst and, having dragged the sergeant out again, commenced to flog the men who had protected him. This sergeant when he reached camp was brought into Mahomed Russi's tent and flogged again, while several of the senior NCOs of the Regiment were brought up and warned that they also would be flogged if anything similar happened again.

No rations were issued today, so to sleep hungry once more.

Sunday, 14 May. We continued to march at the usual hour and arrived at Ctesiphon about 1600 hours. This was the most tedious march we had done so far; from Lajj we had to follow the big bend of the river to avoid the marshes, and it would often look as if we were marching aimlessly, for the great arch of Ctesiphon would sometimes appear about a mile away and shortly afterwards be hardly discernible in the mist; during this time we could see the column stretching for miles behind us and could not discern the rear, this great length being caused by the escort making continual gaps between Units and preventing them from closing up. Today we went again without rations.

On Monday, 15 May we marched again at the usual hour, and were agreeably surprised to halt at 0840 hours, quite delightful after our really hard march on the previous day. Today we received some rations as follows: six small sheep and one goat for the Battalion (roughly 250 men), with three biscuits and one little piece of stinking, mouldy chupattie, but no wood to cook the sheep was issued. While rations were being drawn some of the ration party picked up some bits of biscuit which had fallen out of the bags on to the ground. Lieutenant Mahomed Russie saw this and gave Turkish soldiers an order which caused them to search the whole of the ration party. They found three men with bits of biscuit in their pockets and these were taken to Mahomed Russi, who personally flogged all three giving them each twenty lashes on the back, this after being without food for three days . . .

Tuesday, 16 May we started off at the usual time and halted at 1130 hours on the right bank of the Dialia River about eight miles from its junction with the Tigris. We had seen the Minarets of Baghdad practically the whole of the time after crossing the Dialia . . .

We continued our march at the usual time on Wednesday, 17 May and after proceeding some distance along the bank of the Dialia River, we began to move towards Baghdad. We encountered several stretches of water and pieces of marsh which we had to wade through, these latter were particularly tiring to us.

About 1000 hours we entered the outskirts of the city. Here our escorts commenced to hustle us, continually charging us without any regard as to who they hit over. When we passed the German Consulate, the German crew of the *Goeben* were standing on the steps and outside. As we passed they commenced to spit at us and threw stones. This seemed to give Lieutenant Mohamed Russi an idea for he halted his horse close to the flank of the Column and commenced to lash every man he could reach with his whip.

When he became tired of this he suddenly galloped his horse

until he arrived at the rear of the Indian Troops who were marching immediately in front of us; here he charged his horse amongst the Indians, and taking them in the backs knocked a large number down, at the same time using his whip as usual. Several of the Indians who were knocked down could hardly walk and had to be assisted along by their comrades; and so we continued through Baghdad, quite a triumphant procession from the Turkish point of view.

Instead of taking the road direct along the river front we were hustled all through the bazaars where we received every possible insult. Spitting at us was their chief delight, and needless to say plenty of cameras were levelled at us. After wandering around the bazaars for a couple of hours we crossed the Bridge of Boats and eventually arrived near the railway station where we bivouacked . . .

No move took place that day, but the whole of the day we were pestered by a motley collection representing, I suppose, the residents of Baghdad; Arabs, Turks, Greeks, Jews, Armenians, and a host of other nationalities who wanted to finger every article we were wearing. It was a hard and weary job watching our little bit of belongings; we had to sit on them to avoid losing the lot. I believe our escort did a roaring trade at so much per head to the populace, by letting them in to inspect us in the bivouac at close quarters and steal what they could manage. Many were the bitter outcries when men left their kits for a few minutes and came back to find that everything had disappeared.

At about 0400 hours on Friday, 19 May we were routed out, knocked and kicked off to the station and put into open trucks. The train started at 0600 hours, and we were accommodated at about 40 men to each truck, well packed together. As the morning passed the heat became intense, and as our small supply of water decreased, so our discomfort increased. We arrived at our journey's end at about noon and were heartily glad to get out of the train. We had seen a strikingly gilded dome for a considerable distance during the journey, and saw by the name on the station that it was Samarra we had reached . . .

Shortly after 0100 hours on Sunday, 21 May a terrific storm burst over us. It commenced with a sand storm, which caused a great amount of discomfort, but it was nothing to what we felt when the rain came on, which continued for several hours, leaving us in the early hours of the morning wet, miserable and shivering, and our spirits at the lowest possible level. During the course of the storm, quite a number of men had their blankets and helmets blown away, mostly into the river, and in consequence were left without any covering for their heads to protect them from the blazing sun.

Except for those without helmets, we were glad when the sun put in an appearance to enable us to dry ourselves as well as put some warmth into our wretched bodies . . .

On Monday, 22 May we were told to get ready for the march again . . . We commenced at 1730 hours, and continued marching until 0130 hours on Tuesday, 23rd, when a halt was called and we promptly lay down as we were, on the pathway, just the same as we were marching, and just as promptly fell asleep. After what seemed only a few minutes we heard the usual chorus of whips and '*Yellah*'*s*', but my watch said 0400 hours, so it must have been two and a half hours sleep we had had. The escort commenced to harry us, using whips, sticks and the butts of their rifles to keep us moving; it looked as if they were in a hurry to get along, but I found out after that it was only to make sure that we should not communicate with the column which had to follow us, being afraid that we might compare notes on our treatment.

As the day wore on the heat became intense and so did our thirst, and the men who lost their helmets suffered awful agonies. At 1400 hours we reached the village of Tekhrit, exhausted and quite willing to quit this life if we could only see a quick way out.

Our bivouac was the foreshore of the river, a place absolutely designed for us, as it was covered with small boulders and wet sand. The town towered on the top of the cliffs above and many of the sympathetic inhabitants dropped rocks on to us as a welcome. Our sanitary arrangements were delightful; our latrines were two yards from the bivouac, and any man getting there was promptly stoned by our friends in the village . . .

At 1700 hours the escort came galloping through the camp shouting their usual '*Yellahs*'. We were kept moving till 0800 hours on 25 May, when we bivouacked again on the banks of the Tigris. The men who had lost their helmets in the storm at Samarra felt the effects of the heat greatly during the day, the only protection for their heads being a towel twisted up in turban fashion, which did not give nearly sufficient protection. Several men had also lost their boots; these had been stolen from them while they slept. Their sufferings were terrible, their feet were horribly cut about before they had been long on the march.

This stealing of boots was certainly done by our escort. To prevent mine being stolen I used to wear them when I was asleep; it made one's feet very bad but that was better than marching without any at all. Lieutenant Mahomed Russi, on being told that his men were stealing our boots, jeered at us and, through an interpreter, told us it would do us all good to march bare-footed . . .

During Friday, 26 May Enver Pasha* passed the bivouac on the way from his inspection of the Iraq Front. He interviewed a few of the Native Moslems, but would not speak to any Englishman . . .

We marched at 1700 hours until 0930 hours on 27 May. It was a horrid march, mostly through sand, and well away from the river. Our escort knew what the route was like, for on the way during previous days they had obtained goat skins which they

* Turkish War Minister.

carried under the girths of their ponies, but never a drink would they give to any of us prisoners. They treated their ponies as bad for the poor brutes were left saddled up in the sun all day with their tongues hanging out.

We continued the march at 1800 hours, and eventually reached the Tigris again at 0730 hours on Sunday, 28 May. I have since heard many speak of the distance covered in those two days, the generally accepted distance being 66 kilometres, which I should think was correct or thereabouts . . .

Sergt-Major Thompson was flogged by Mahomed Russi this day. At the end of the march, this Turkish officer shouted something to Thompson in Turkish or Arabic which apparently was an order to double to him. Thompson, not being able to understand him, continued to walk. Mahomed Russi promptly ordered some of the escort to seize him which they did, and Mahomed Russi flogged him himself; at the time Thompson was very ill with dysentery.

On Monday, 29 May we were able to rest during the morning, and we washed ourselves and our clothes. The name of the village we heard was Silgit, somewhere near the old city of Assur. During the day our Indian followers were removed from us; three separate columns were formed, one British, one Mahomedan, and one Hindu . . .

Wednesday, 31 May. The yarn goes round the bivouac that we have only two more marches to Mosul, and I for one sincerely hope so. I think almost all the men are done up and do not appear to be able to march much further. The way we have been driven along is appalling. Our escort, the Kurdish Cavalry, would hardly be termed humane by the most vivid imagination, using sticks, whips and the butt end of their rifles on any poor devil who is unfortunate enough to fall out for the purposes of nature or exhaustion . . .

Friday, 2 June. We commenced to march at 0500 hours, and

continued until midnight. The road was very rough, with very sharp flints shewing up, and many were the screams of the men without boots when their feet and flints came into collision. It was quite bad enough for us with boots; we twisted our ankles, and had a hard time to keep going, the road being very hilly. At about 2200 hours we saw far below us the lights of a city, and so we presumed that they were the lights of Mosul, which turned out to be correct . . .

Saturday, 3 June. On arrival in Mosul we were parked on the public square in front of the Serai, where we remained on view to the population, who flocked around to see such strange, half-starved people, quite a novel sight for them. Extra guards were posted over us to impress the population, although just at that time I do not think there was any great need for them.

Our rations were more ample today, consisting of half a loaf of bread and one chupattie, and about six o'clock in the evening we received about four tablespoons of stew, little enough, but the best we had tasted for months. It was much better than our mule flesh stews of Kut; we actually had a little mutton or goat flesh floating about in it. The bread and chupattie had been a whole day's work to draw. The ration party was entirely surrounded by guards before moving off, and when we proceeded into the Serai. On reaching there we were shut up into a small room, very dark and hardly room to stand. Here we were kept for an hour, then we were taken out to a corner, hemmed in by guards, and kept standing in the sun for four hours.

One good thing I saw during this time was one of the officers who commanded one of the Kurdish Cavalry Squadrons of our escort being led across the square of the Serai in irons. He was one of the most vile and cruel beasts that it was possible to meet, and we rejoiced to see him going through the mill instead of putting us through it. We slept on the square, but it was vastly necessary to watch and guard our little bit of property . . .

Sunday, 4 June . . . About 1900 hours we had to pack up our belongings and move into the Serai. Apparently we had been on show long enough, but when we were shown inside and stowed away in the dungeons there, we would have preferred to have been outside in the open. The place swarmed with lice, and we were not allowed outside for the purpose of nature. While we were bivouacked on the square we had been allowed to go to the river bank for water; here the place we had to get it from was just below the hospital where all filth and old droppings were emptied. One dipped a canteen in the water and drank, looked at the spot where it was taken from and saw excreta floating along on the top. How any of us escaped enteric or some worse disease seems a wonder. For my part, my stomach gave me great pain, and I had a bad attack of diarrhoea; this was awful in a closed building with no latrines at night.

Monday, 6 June . . . About 1630 hours we were off on the march again, this time it was only English in our column. The march this day was not very desperate, except that the road was very rocky, which was very bad for the men without boots, although the majority of men who had no boots were left behind at Mosul practically dying. Several others were left there and very few survived. We had dropped a sprinkling of men along the road all the way along the march; these men had fallen out overcome by exhaustion and were never seen again. If they did not die by the roadside the Arabs would very soon be along and cut their throats for the sake of their boots . . .

During the day we could look back on the River Tigris and see Mosul in the distance. We were on the hills surrounding the city. Although at the time I did not know it, this day was to be my last to look on the Tigris, and before many days were gone we looked back on the days when we were able to drink, bathe and enjoy the muddy waters of the river . . .

Tuesday, 7 June . . . At 1700 hours we were hustled off on the march again, feeling as if we would drop before many paces were taken; however, we managed to keep it up and eventually halted about midnight. Whenever these halts took place we never knew for how long they were for, so we became past masters in the art of quickness in unrolling and rolling our blanket; almost as soon as we heard a shout, our blanket would be rolled and on the back, pack-fashion, while as soon as we halted the blanket was unstrapped and we rolled in it, with never a thought as to removing our clothes or boots. This latter was too dangerous a proceeding as I have mentioned before.

Thursday, 8 June . . . We commenced to march at 1600 hours, and just as we were about to start, three men of the Battalion collapsed. I went to the Commandant, Mahomed Russi, and asked his aid to get the men looked after, but instead I was threatened with a flogging and chased off back to where the Battalion was. We had to leave these three dying in the desert, without any help, and the only drop of water (if they could have managed to drag their limbs to it) was nearly half a mile away and salt at that. These men never came on, and I was told by an Englishman who came on some weeks later, that there were three skeletons on this spot. We had been comparing notes of the march and, from what he told me, it looked as if the poor fellows had been trying to drag themselves down to the water but had died, or possibly been killed for their boots and bits of kit by wandering Arabs.

We had not been very long on the march when we encountered a heavy thunderstorm. The little water we could wring out of our clothes as we marched was very refreshing, but we were wet through as well as our packs, which added to the weight to be carried and to our discomfort. About an hour later another storm broke and it was very hard to battle against it, but we had to go, our escort saw to that; they were mounted and their ponies had to do the marching for them.

Before starting we had been ordered to fill some mussacks, to be carried on a couple of camels, as this was to be a long march. This was done and about midnight a halt was called, and parties were called from each unit to draw water from the camels. The remainder were told not to untie their packs as it was only a few minutes halt. I went with the party to draw the water, but on arrival at the camels we found the mussacks flat on the camels' backs, bone dry, and several slits in their sides where apparently knives had been pushed in so that we might not get any water. This apparently pleased the Commandant, Mahomed Russi, as he was laughing and chuckling with glee as he peered in our crestfallen faces to see how we liked the sight of our loss of the much needed water . . .

Friday, 9 June. No stream or well of any description was along this tract and the sufferings of the men were awful. One man I saw, who on coming to a little depression in the ground which showed traces of the storm the night before, drop on his knees and commence to scoop the earth out almost like a dog. As soon as he had cleared out a little sand he clapped his mouth to the sand in the hopes of being able to suck out a little water, and so quench his awful thirst. I am afraid he was not very successful. However, everything has its end, and so did the march for we halted beside, what I thought at the time, was the most perfect stream of running water it was possible to behold in any part of the world. I am afraid we drank well if not wisely.

We were very tired and worn out, but with as few men as possible I had to go and draw what rations there were to be had. These had to be fetched from nearly two miles away, and the poor fellows with me could hardly drag their limbs along; but they knew it was either a case of dragging themselves on or the whole Regiment (or what was left of it) dying of starvation. We received some barley meal, peas, and two goats, with a very little wood. I saw a couple of cauldrons, and taking the chance of a flogging (which was usual if one asked for anything) begged the loan of them from the Commandant. At first he looked as if the flogging was to be my portion, but after a time he relented, and I marched back in triumph with two cauldrons and the rations.

After a good deal of trouble, I managed to persuade some good fellows to kill the goats, and others to assist in cutting up and getting the pot filled. The goats were killed and skinned with table and pocket knives; any other knives had been taken away from us long ago. I am afraid the poor goats' death was not exactly painless, but we could not help that; they had to go into the pots for our own sakes. These two pots were cooked and ready by about 1900 hours, when I doled out to each little group in the Battalion. If it had been issued raw it would have been insignificant, but cooked together it made quite a passable small meal . . .

Saturday, 10 June. I was mighty near getting a hammering just as we commenced the march at 1700 hours. The Kurdish Bas-Choush (Sergeant-Major) was on his horse on the other side of the stream, and bawled across for us to go over at that point. Here the water was waist-deep, which would have made us all very wet and uncomfortable for the march. As I was leading the Regiment I pretended not to hear the shouting but continued downstream to where there happened to be stepping stones. We all got over without mishap or wetting, but as soon as we were on the top of the bank, the Bas-Choush made a fierce rush at me; he was on his horse but I managed to dodge him. He did this several times but failed to lay hold of me; at the finish he brought his horse to a standstill and looked at me, grinding his teeth with rage and threatening me with a fine hiding when we halted. However, when we did halt I suppose he had forgotten, or he wanted to sleep himself; anyway, I had no further trouble on this account from him.

Sunday, 11 June . . . As soon as we reached camp we had to go off to draw rations. This consisted of about half a pound of barley meal, four ounces of crushed wheat, with a little salt, ghi and a stick of wood per man. It took me four hours to draw. I was on the move all the time we were supposed to be halted, and if it had not been for my messmates I should have fared rather badly for want of food. I felt as tired as a dog might feel who had been on the roam all night when we marched off again at 1800 hours, but I had to make the best of it and keep moving with the remainder. Many times during the march I fell asleep while marching, and at any little check in the column, I walked straight into the man ahead of me. When I woke again I was cursed for it many times, but that did not prevent me doing it again almost at once, and I really could not help it, I was tired out. We halted again at about midnight.

Thursday, 15 June. We commenced to march at 1600 hours. I was feeling very unwell when we started this march, and came over worse as we moved on. Eventually I had to drop out, and before long the column had almost passed me; seeing this I commenced to gird up my loins to move along. Just then a Kurd came along on his horse and commenced to hammer into me. However, before I had taken many paces, another of the escort rode up, and I suddenly heard a voice shouting my name. I answered at once, and before another second the Kurd who was letting into me was on the flat of his back, having been knocked off his pony by one terrific hit. This had been done by the Bas-Choush of our immediate escort; he had it seemed known me by my walk.

I was mighty thankful for this at the time, but of course, being what he was, he had another end in view. So as I plodded along the track he came up on his pony and asked me in Arabic and the sign language we used to sort out, what was the matter with me. I told him I was unwell in the stomach, and he promptly wanted me to put my kit containing my blanket and my other few necessities on his pony. I as promptly refused, knowing full well that once he had hold of it I should never see it again. So I struggled on as best as I could, and after a hard pull I managed to catch up the Battalion. I could well understand what the other poor devils who had fallen behind had had to put up with, more so as many were undoubtedly much worse treated than I was.

Friday, 16 June . . . I was feeling particularly rough today, so much so that I could not get myself off to draw rations; however my good friend Sergeant-Major Dribbs did it for me. This was the only time during the march that I had not been able to go to the spot where rations were issued and see that our men did not go short as far as was possible . . .

Saturday, 17 June . . . During the day we were issued with a loaf of bread for our day's ration. I should think it weighed about 12 ounces, and in colour was black, green, grey, blue and in fact every colour one could think of, and if it had not been for our hunger I am quite sure it would all have been thrown away. I feel much better today, but my friend Thompson, with whom I have been sharing all things during the march, begins to feel unwell, and complains of dysentery. Our bivouac today is situated on the village filth bed; smells awful, and to lie down or sit down is repulsive.

Sunday, 18 June . . . We were ordered to draw two days rations. We were told that this was to last us until we reached the *chemin-de-fer*. I think this news has put a certain amount of new life into the majority of men, but of course a few croakers say there is no such thing as the Baghdad Railway . . .

Tuesday, 20 June. We halted at 0530 hours by the side of the lake outside the village of Ras-Al-Ain, but before we had time to settle we were shifted off to a spot near the Railway Station. When we moved from the station I had the job of checking the column with the Commandant, Mahomed Russi. I had picked up a smattering of Turkish counting and he knew it.

The number we have left looks appalling; no one will ever know how many were left on the roadside to die. While on this counting process I could see the Hindu column bivouacked on the hill side. They had been marching a day ahead of us, and their treatment had, I believe, been worse than ours. They had been treated worse than us when we had been all together, kicked and knocked about far more than either the British or the Mahomedans; although God knows we were treated bad enough.

One would have thought that the Mahomedan Kurds, as co-religionists, would have shown a trifle of feeling to their brother Indian Mahomedans in their religious observances, but it was not so. Many an Indian I have seen kneeling towards Mecca at sunset, and on any one of our escort seeing them thus, he would at once ride up and commence to flog them whilst still on their knees at their devotions, and eventually forcing the poor devils to get up. Needless to say one never saw the Kurds at any devotions.

While we were waiting outside the Station we saw a German train of motor lorries and men arrive; except for those in Baghdad, the Germans we had met on the march had treated us fairly decently. The Turks we had met had been very much the reverse, it being very common for them on meeting us on the march to strike our men with their clubbed rifles.

We entrained at 1700 hours at Ras-Al-Ain Station, but it was not until 1830 hours that we started off. We were this time accommodated in open trucks. I cannot remember now how many we had, but I well remember that we had just room to sit down by keeping our knees up to our chins, so it was quite impossible to lie down at all. The worst aspect was for the poor fellows who were ill, many of them with dysentery. Sergeant-Major Thompson was a case like this. I had been sharing everything with him on the march and of course tried to make him as comfortable as I could, but our escort would not allow anyone to leave the trucks when the train stopped, even for the purposes of nature, so that before the night was out the state of the trucks was to say the least of it awful. It was not until the train stopped at about 0800 hours on 21 June, at the Junction for Allepo, that we were allowed to get out.

During the night many had been the alarms of fire, as the engine was burning wood, and so was continually casting a whole crowd of sparks over us. The result was that many parts of the men's clothing and blankets were set alight. Several times it was a hard job to put it out, and to top all, the escort, when they saw us struggling with the fire, would laugh at us from the little brake hutches on the end of each truck in which they were accommodated. Many of the fires of course occurred on men who could hardly move on account of sickness.

We were on the move again from this Junction at about 0900 hours and still in the open trucks, so we soon began to feel the effects of the heat as much as we had felt the cold during the night. At 1730 hours we arrived at Islahie, the then railhead on the eastern side of the Ammanus (or Anti Taurus) Mountains. One particular incident I noticed while we were detraining. A man who was frightfully sick had been helped out of the train by his comrades, who then scrambled for their own belongings. The sick man, after standing up for a few minutes, fell down and could not rise; a couple of other men assisted him up, but were of course very slow in moving with such a burden. This upset the escort, and a number of them forced the two who were helping the sick man to let go, and as soon as we had moved along for a little way, they commenced to belabour the poor fellow with sticks. The Commandant, Mahomed Russi, stood by with his revolver in his hand, and also had several of the escort ready with their rifles, to see that we did not return and interfere. Whilst this was happening and we were taking backward glances, we were being pushed clear of the Station to the open country where we were to bivouac.

On the opposite side of the line was a big German camp, and I believe it was through their good interests that a medical inspection took place. This resulted in 39 men of the Regiment being found too ill to proceed. My friend Sergeant-Major Thompson was one of these. Partings of this sort were heart-breaking as we could not tell if we should ever meet again. I heard long after that he died at Adana. However, at the time he could not have marched a mile, so we divided our belongings, including a little money, and parted. I was informed by a man of the party who was left behind that shortly after we had moved the Turks came around and searched every man, and finding a couple of Mejidiehs* on Thompson, took not only that, but all his spare kit, including his blanket from him . . .

Thursday, 22 June. We commenced to march again at 0100 hours. We very soon found ourselves going up into the mountains, and until reaching the crest of the hill at 0630 hours, we had only had one halt of five minutes, and we were being driven along at top speed. At the top of the hill we had another five minutes halt, and on its completion we were almost driven at the double downhill until 0940 hours; anyone who hung behind had the usual lashings from the escort.

We bivouacked near a pretty little hill village, but of course we were not allowed into the village. This had been the rule with our escort all the way; they would never let us into the villages, but if they could buy anything themselves they would offer some of it (i.e. eatables) to us at very enhanced prices, but as no one had much money they did not sell much . . .

All through the remainder of the night we travelled up and down hill, and shortly after dawn on Friday, 23 June, when on the crest of a rise, we could see traces of the railway in the valley below. We halted about 0900 hours a little distance from the Railway Station at Mamoure . . .

Saturday, 24 June. We entrained at Mamoure Station at 0730 hours, and reached Adana at about 1230 hours where we

* Silver coins.

detrained. Evidently something was wrong, the way the Commandant behaved. He rushed about and waved his arms all over the place, and did not appear to know what he was doing. After hanging about this station for a couple of hours we were bundled back into the train, and soon started to go back the way we had come. Rumour was rife among all the troops as to why we were returning. Allepo or Damascus seemed our favourite destination, but a few knew that we were for railway construction, although no one knew where. They had heard this from our escort at Adana; however, no one cared as long as it was a third class ride and not a third class walk. We reached Mamoure about 2000 hours.

Sunday, 25 June . . . About midday we were told to pack up and move to another camp. We expected to be in the vicinity, but instead we were very soon marching back into the mountains, and a long dreary march it was. The going was particularly tough, especially when we reached a side track where we turned up into a long wooded valley. Before reaching this turning, while going up a very steep portion of the road, a man who was unable to keep up fell out to the side of the road. The Commandant coming up on his pony at this time commenced to lash at the man with his whip. Finding the man too much exhausted to go on, he shouted to one of the escort, who came up and promptly clubbed the man on the head with his rifle, then getting off his pony, dragged him to the side of the track and pushed him over the side. This man was never seen again by any of his comrades.

I was particularly done up on this march, as I had a very bad touch of dysentery and could hardly keep going. However, I managed to pull through somehow, and about midnight we reached some buildings where we halted in the roadway. These buildings I knew very well before long as Bagtsche Station. Here we were issued with one loaf of bread, black and only half baked, and were told that we were to commence work on railway construction . . .

Monday, 26 June. About 0900 hours we were herded together and taken a little distance from the village. Here we found several railway officials who called for the senior of each unit in turn. I went up for the Regiment to see what was happening. The first question was: How many men have you, including everyone? It was a terrible surprise to even myself when I answered 140. We had left Kut over 250 strong. The balance had been left mostly on the road either dead or dying, and among those who remained was not one fit man; all were practically skeletons, while many were almost fit to die with dysentery and various other complaints.

If the Engineers had taken the trouble to have had us medically examined with a view to the amount of work we were able to perform, it would probably have saved them a lot of trouble, but the great thing was any labour, even the poorest, was valuable as the railway had to be finished. After a lot of talk we were sent off in the company of a subordinate Engineer, and he led us back the way we had arrived last night until . . .

Harvey's narrative breaks off at this point, but his original diary entries for the next three months are appended. They indicate that 32 more men of the Battalion died while working on the railway during July and August. Harvey himself, who was twice threatened with flogging for standing up for his men, became very ill with malaria but managed to keep clear of the hospital, of which he writes:

There is practically no medicine to be obtained, and a dog is better treated in England than our poor fellows are in hospital here. When a man dies he is dragged out without even a sheet to cover him, and on the side of the hill above the hospital they scrape a few inches of dirt above the bodies, consequently the dogs and jackals dig up the bodies after burial and half devour them as soon as it is dark.

Three isolated diary entries for January, 1917, suggest that the survivors of what must be accounted the most terrible ordeal suffered by First World War PoWs were at last settled down in relatively decent billets and receiving mails from home. Harvey's last entry reads: 'Wednesday, 31 January. Received an issue of bacon last night, and chocolates (Nestle's Milk) yesterday. Had the bacon cold for breakfast this morning, nice change.'

In the official history of the Dorsetshire Regiment Harvey rates only a passing mention. From the Ministry of Defence's voluminous records of servicemen of two world wars he emerges as just another name: Born Taunton, Somerset, November, 1885. Enlisted 1 July, 1904, aged 18 years 8 months. 5ft 4½ins, light brown hair, hazel eyes. Next of kin: father, William. World War I: Mesoptomia from October, 1914 to April, 1916. Prisoner of War April, 1916 to November, 1918 . . .

Harvey would have remained a shadowy figure had not the curator of the regimental museum in Dorchester suggested the names of two men whom he thought might provide clues: a retired colonel and a Chelsea Pensioner. Against all the odds, they were able to provide much more than clues. Both had known Harvey well, almost certainly the last two still alive who remembered him at all.

Colonel Robert Goff, OBE, MC, at his home near Piltdown, Sussex, was intrigued to learn of the diary and delighted to talk about a man he regarded as an epitome of all that was best in Army life. He had first met Harvey when he joined the Regiment in Bangalore, Southern India, in 1919, and became a close friend until the time he was killed in October, 1921.

'Through sheer strength of personality Harvey had risen through the ranks to become Quartermaster Lieutenant, a very big shot in a regiment,' he recalls. 'I was a good deal his junior—I was 21 in 1919, Harvey 34. But we became great friends, together with John Hewick, who I now see was responsible for getting the diary printed and who wrote the introduction. We three were very much together.

'Harvey stood out as unique in the Regiment. He was a thickset man, with a fine face, a man who knew his own mind, a man who inspired respect, even awe, but who was very much loved. For some reason he was always known as "Kate". Though from a working-class background, he had an educated voice and was the type who would get on with public school men. Had he lived he would undoubtedly have risen to Quartermaster Colonel. He was an abstemious drinker, a pipe smoker, and had no interests outside the Army. The Army was what he lived for.

'Kut and its aftermath was not a subject that any survivor was frightfully keen to talk about. The only time I recall Harvey referring to his experiences was once when we were discussing the psychological aspects of warfare. "You'd be amazed how easily and quickly the animal side of human nature comes out," Harvey said, but he did not expand. I imagine that when he came out of it all he told himself, "That's that and I'm going to try and forget it." But I still think it shameful that he received no decoration – a DCM at least.'

Colonel Goff was not present when Harvey was shot in an ambush, soon afterwards dying of his wounds. Private Ned Burwood saw him shot. More than that, he had been one of the 252 men of the Dorsets in the death march column that Harvey led.

Aged 84 now, still hale and hearty, Burwood is one of the 400 old soldiers who proudly sport the distinctive uniform of the Chelsea Pensioner at their barrack-like quarters at the Royal Hospital, Chelsea. Most mornings you can find whole squads of them quaffing their pre-dinner pints round long wooden tables in the spacious mess, an exclusive brotherhood of 'living histories'. There is not much harking back to battles long ago, but the memories are still there. Ned Burwood's eyes lit up at mention of RQMS 'Kate' Harvey.

For 15 years after the end of his army service in 1935 Burwood had trudged the pavements of Harrow as a postman, but he gives the impression now of never having left the Army. It is his element. And it is as an old soldier that he talks (even addressing one as 'sir') as he revives memories of that nightmare trek across desert and mountain in the steps of a born leader of men.

'He was an upstanding little fella, sir, a gentleman through and through. You kept your place with him but he was not a bumptious fella – he was a soldier, one of the best. To me his memory still lingers. I can see him now at the head of the column, weak as he was himself, or coming back when we were straggling perhaps two miles with long gaps between, coaxing us along: "Come on, boys, come on, come on, keep up."

'It's difficult to explain what we were like even before the march after five months on starvation rations. Too far gone to worry about what was happening, no incentive to live. It was "Kate" Harvey — and thoughts of the family at home — that kept us going, with those Kurdish swine lashing at us with their bulls' pizzles and butting us with their rifle butts. I'd shoot the buggers now if I had my way.

'I was bastinadoed once for pinching from an Arab pony's rations. They made us water the ponies and feed them their maize. One day I pinched a handful and was spotted putting it in my pocket. I got seven strokes of the bastinado for that. They laid you on your back and tied a stick between your legs. Seven strokes across the bottom of your feet. Painful? Worst punishment in the world, sir.'

Burwood produces a tattered, much-thumbed copy of a 'Statement of Maltreatment' he made shortly after the war when he was stationed in India. It has particular reference to the sadistic Commandant, Lieutenant Mahomed Russi, and was one of a number of similar testimonies from PoWs produced at his trial. Burwood believes that the trial was held at the Tower of London, but that at the end of it 'the swine got away with it'.

'. . . I saw Mahomed Russi illtreat several of my Comrades. One case in particular is that of Pte Hobbs, of the 2nd Dorsetshire Regiment, whom this Officer had ordered to be tied up by the hands, handcuffed fashion, and tied to the saddle of the Arab escort's horse, and made to keep up with the Rider, he was treated in this manner for two days. There were also several Blue Jackets, who were very weak and suffering from dysentery, and could not walk, and were tied to camels without helmets and dragged along, I personally saw TWO of them when the Camels halted taken off DEAD.

'I should also mention the case of Pte Whitehead of the 1/4th Battalion, The Hants Regiment. Whilst he was riding a donkey, owing to him being unable to walk, the Arab Escort seemed to enjoy the flogging him, and the Commandant of the Escort knew this was being done. The Commandant was Mahomed Russi. This Officer was located recently in the prisoner of war camp at Bellery . . .'

Burwood adds a footnote to the case of Private Whitehead, not used in his statement because he was not an eyewitness. 'Whitehead and another boy of the Hants Regiment had been taken into a Kurdish tent and sexually molested. He died later. Poor little Whitehead was only small, about 7 stone and 5ft 3, quite a boy. There was quite a lot of that went on.'

It is rarely that Ned Burwood has unburdened himself of such memories. 'Funny thing, sir, you can believe me or disbelieve me, but even at the Kut reunion dinners we used to have in London you never heard nothing about what we'd been through. We'd have a sing-song, drink and all that, but we never harked back, too awful. And I never talked about it with "Kate" Harvey when we were in India together. Not that we were on speaking terms like that, him being an officer. It was "Good morning, Burwood," "Good morning, sir." An Army man, sir, you can't beat them.'

It was on 1 October, 1921, that Burwood was on a routine patrol with Harvey at a village called Vadapuram in Malabar. The Moplah Rebellion was at its height, one of those local uprisings, little noticed at the time, that were inexorably leading, where Kut had begun, to the dissolution of the British Raj. These patrols were fraught with danger, and there was an added undertone of horror that echoed back to Kut. It was not uncommon to come across a British soldier, killed in an ambush, left lying in the roadway as an awful warning of Indian retribution, his genitals cut off and stuck in his mouth. The Arab scavengers had done likewise along the death route from Kut.

The patrol in which Harvey and Burwood were marching again together was deploying cautiously through a coconut grove, 'We heard shots,' says Burwood, trying to focus his mind's eye on that distant spot all those years ago. ' "Kate" Harvey dropped. Him and a bloke named McGill. It was a sniper up a coconut tree got them. We brought him down alright. McGill was killed outright. Harvey died soon after. We had to move on and, as far as I remember, they were buried there. We couldn't have carried them far, because of the heat, you understand.'

Ned Burwood pauses, temporarily isolated from the old familiar faces and voices around him in the mess of this comfortable billet where he will end his days. 'A miserable end for a man like "Kate" Harvey, when you think of it. To me always a gentleman. A lovely fella.'

END